The Regiments of the British Indian Army 1895–1947

The Army of the Crown

Baudouin Ourari

Artwork by Mike Chappell and Bruno Mugnai

Helion & Company

Helion & Company Limited
Unit 8 Amherst Business Centre
Budbrooke Road
Warwick
CV34 5WE
England
Tel. 01926 499 619
Email: info@helion.co.uk
Website: www.helion.co.uk
Twitter: @helionbooks
Visit our blog http://blog.helion.co.uk/

Published by Helion & Company 2019

Designed and typeset by Farr out Publications, Wokingham, Berkshire
Cover designed by Farr out Publications, Wokingham, Berkshire
Printed by IBI, Dulles VA, USA

ISBN 978-1-911628-95-8

British Library Cataloguing-in-Publication Data.
A catalogue record for this book is available from the British Library.

For details of other military history titles published by Helion & Company Limited contact the above address, or visit our website: http://www.helion.co.uk.

We always welcome receiving book proposals from prospective authors.

Contents

List of abbreviations

ABC	Army Bearer Corps
ABN	Airborne
AD	Armoured Division
AF(I)	Auxiliary Force (India)
AHC	Army Hospital Corps
BLI	Bengal Light Infantry
BNI	Bengal Native Infantry
By.	Battery
CD	Cavalry Division
DCO	Duke (Duchess) of Connaught's Own
DCO	Duke (Duchess) of Cornwall's Own
DYO	Duke (Duchess) of York's Own
FC	Frontier Corps
FF	Frontier Force
ICO	Indian Commissioned Officer
ID	Infantry Division
IDF	Indian Defence Force
IECO	Indian Emergency Commissioned Officer
IEF	Indian Expeditionary Force
ISF	Indian State Force
IST	Imperial Service Troops
ITF	Indian Territorial Force
IVF	Indian Volunteer Force
KCIO	King's Commissioned Indian Officer
KEO	King Edward's Own
KGO	King George's Own
KIOO	King's Indian Orderly Officer
LI	Light Infantry
NWF	North West Frontier
PAVO	Prince Albert Victor's Own
PIF	Punjab Irregular Force
PWO	Prince of Wales's Own
QO	Queen's Own
QVO	Queen's Victoria' Own
VCO	Viceroy's Commissioned Officer

Glossary

Alkalak	long coat worn by horsemen
assami	amount of money to compensate silladar
bahadur	champion, hero
cummerbund	waist sash
dacoït	an outlaw
durbar	assembly, government
hessian	boot reaching to the knee
izzat	honour, loyalty
jodhpurs	riding breeches
kaki (khaki)	from Persian: "dust"
kula	rigid headdress worn under the lungi
kurta	loose frock reaching to the knees
lascar	camp follower
lungi	turban, headdress
moghul	ruling dynasty à 1857
poshteen	coat of sheepskin
pugri, pagri	cloth worn around the head
puttee	cloth worn round the leg
pyjamas	loose trousers worn by cavalrymen
raj	state, empire
rissalah	any formed body of horse
sabretache	pocket suspended to sword belt
salutri	veterinary officer
sepoy	native soldier/infantryman
silladar	a cavalryman owning his horse
sirdar	chief, governor
sowar	cavalryman
tulwar	curved native sword

Acknowledgements

First of all, I want to express my deep admiration and gratitude to Mike Chappell whose talent has been a driving force behind my enthusiasm.

I am indebted to all the authors and works mentioned in the bibliography.

A special thank you has to be given to John Gaylor and Major D. Jackson who have guided me through the Indian Regiment history.

The magnificence of Indian uniforms of the past centuries has been preserved for posterity in the fantastic paintings of Major A. C. Lovett and the outstanding work of W.Y. Carman.

Finally, I want to point out the great website www.britishempire.co.uk which is a goldmine for the 1903 Army of India.

Introduction

The origins of the Indian Army go back to the military units raised by the Honourable East India Company in the 17th century.

The Indian Mutiny of 1857 was a crucial event, because, after it was over, the British government undertook the reforms that gave the Indian Army its definitive character.

During the period from 1895 to 1947, the Indian Army reached the peak of its power and development. During the course of this half-century, an organisation came into being whose members, officers and soldiers alike, all volunteers, were united by a wonderful *esprit de corps*. The unified nature of the Indian Army was never undermined by the push towards nationalism within the people and the political elite.

One of the specific aspects of the Indian Army was the way its recruitment practice was focused mainly on the peoples from the north of the country, who might be called "warlike tribes": Baluchs, Dogras, Garhwalis, Gurkhas, Mers, Pathans, Muslim Punjabis, Rajput and Sikhs. Punjabis alone accounted for half the total manpower. This practice was only effectively modified with the approach of the Second World War, when the need for troops became so great that recruitment bases were extended to other peoples of the sub-continent.

The life and development of the Indian Army is dotted with milestones. We will take a brief look at them in the first part of the book so that the various regiments can be placed in their historical context.

Map

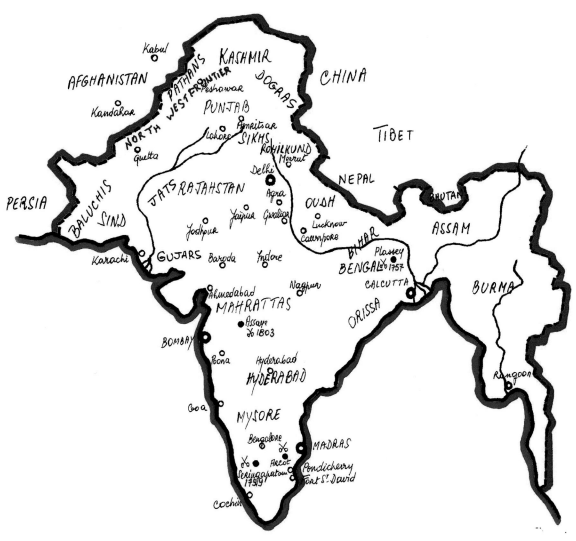

British India, 1850. (Artwork by Baudouin Ourari)

PART I

Historical background

The history of the Indian sub-continent goes back far beyond British colonisation. Way back in the mists of time, the Mauryan Kings had brought structure to large sections of the country. As he advanced through Asia, Alexander the Great had defeated the army of Porus and skirted the North-West of India.

In 262 BC, the emperor Asoka managed to unify two thirds of the country thanks to the mobility of his cavalry. This was followed by a long period of feudal claims, internecine conflicts and rivalry for supremacy.

In 1192 AD, the Turk, Mohammad of Ghur, defeated the emperor Prithviraj Chauhan and, in 1206, established the sultanate of Delhi which lasted until 1526.

In 1526, a small army of Mongols, commanded by Babur, conquered the Hindustan and established the Muslim dynasty of the Mughals. By the end of the 17th century, the declining Mughals were beginning to concede their trading posts to the Europeans and the East India Company was getting a foothold in India that would last for two centuries.

1

The East India Company

1.1 The beginning

In 1661, King Charles II married a Portuguese princess who brought him the city of Bombay as part of her dowry. The King turned control of the city over to the East India Company which already had a number of trading posts in India, and he granted it the right to raise an army, mint currency, dispense justice and declare war. Primarily in Madras (Fort St. George), Charles II gave the Company virtual absolute sovereignty.

The Company then began to extend its territory from the three ports of Bombay, Calcutta and Madras. Created initially for trading purposes, the East India Company (commonly called "John Company") rapidly grew into a formidable political and military enterprise. To ensure the protection of its three main centres, the Company established mercenary units made up of Anglo-Indian troops, but whose officers were only British and no-one else. The first native troops were the two companies of Rajput raised in Bombay in 1683; Bengal and Madras did the same in 1700. In 1756, the Bengal Army, which was by far the largest, had about 20 companies of infantry.

The cavalry did not come into existence until later and was created from the irregular squadrons (*Risallahs*) raised by adventurous officers whose names would remain associated with the future line regiments.

In 1857, nearly 100,000 men served in the Company's Indian formations.

In comparison with the European armies of the time, the Company's "private" army was poorly equipped. Individual weaponry was obsolete, artillery old-fashioned and officers had a much lower salary than civilian administrators of comparable rank. A trading company by definition, the East India Company was very careful to balance the requirements of its military efforts with the budgetary constraints placed upon it.

Well aware of India's immense potential, the British Crown supported and encouraged the Company when it decided to expand its field of action. The civilian and military administrations were grouped under three Presidencies; namely, Bengal (Calcutta), Bombay and Madras, each of which enjoyed autonomy under the authority of the Governor General.

1.2 British supremacy

The Company operated within a specific context: internally, the decay of the Mughal central power paved the way for an upsurge in the power of local sovereigns; regionally, the Company's ambitions were certain to come up against the plans for expansion of other European maritime powers, such as France, the Low Countries and Portugal. Consequently, the Company had twin objectives: to outdo its European rivals, and to benefit from local dissension and arbitration in local conflicts, thus extending its influence.

In 1756, Nawab Siraj-ud-Daulah of Bengal attacked Fort William, which the Company had fortified without his permission. Reinforcements, led by Robert Clive, retook the city in January 1757.

In the meantime, the British had seized the French settlement at Chandernagore. On 23rd June 1757, Siraj was defeated at the Battle of Plassey. He was murdered shortly afterwards and the Company installed his uncle, Mir Jafar, on the throne of Bengal.

In 1760, Mir Kasim succeeded his father-in-law. Taking advantage of the Seven Years' War, the British put an end to French aspirations by defeating their troops at Wandiwash.

In 1764, Mir Kasim, whose aim was to set Bengal free from Company influence, formed an alliance with the Mughal emperor and Nawab Shujah-ud-Daulah of Oudh. The allied troops were defeated at Buxar by the Company's army under Hector Munro.

Finally, a treaty put an end to the war and granted the Company the right to raise taxes in Bengal, Bihar and Orissa. The battles of Plassey and Buxar drew the curtains on 200 years of British rule in India.

1.3 Geographic expansion

The Mysore Wars

Between 1767 and 1799, the Company had to fight against two of its most formidable adversaries.

On the death of the Rajah of Mysore, the commander-in-chief of the army, Hyder Ali, seized power. He then began to expand his territory and, in so doing, encountered the hostility of the neighbouring princes as well as the British.

In 1767, a war broke out between Hyder Ali and the British. The war was to take place in five phases. The first two phases – from 1767 to 1769 and from 1780 to 1782 – were indecisive. In 1782, Hyder Ali died and his son, Tipu Sultan, succeeded him. Tipu signed the Treaty of Mangalore with the British, but this treaty would give no satisfaction to either party.

In 1787, Tipu attacked Travancore over which the Rajah disagreed with him about sovereignty. The British supported the Rajah and marched on Tipu's capital of Seringapatam. Commanded by Cornwallis, the Company's army took Bangalore and laid siege to Seringapatam. Tipu was forced to sign a treaty that allowed the British and their allies to share half of the territory of Mysore between them.

In 1798, Lord Wellesley was appointed Governor-General. He institutionalised a system that gave the Company the right of protection over princes who considered themselves in danger. In exchange, the British would maintain troops on the protected territory.

Eager to reclaim his lost territory, Tipu sought to forge an alliance with France and the Company used it as a pretext to attack Mysore. Mysore's army was defeated at Sedaseer and Malvelly. Tipu withdrew to Seringapatam where he was killed when the city was captured on 4 May 1799. The defeat marked the destruction of Mysore's state.

The main stages of British expansion during the final sixty years of the Company are summed up by Lieutenant-General Menzies:

1792-1801	Extension of the control of Madras presidency over territories that had previously been under Mysore's rule: Tangore/ Hyderabad/ Carnatic.
1800-1810	The Bengal presidency taken away from the Nawab of Oudh: large portions of Oudh/Agra territory around Delhi, and assumes the administration of Orissa.
1816-1820	The Bengal presidency expanded over Gurhwal, Kumoan, Narbada, Ajmer and Merwara. The Bombay presidency annexed territories of western India which were vassals of Maratha.
1826	Burma ceded to Arakan, part of Asssam and Tenasserim, to the presidency of Bengal.

After this came the main annexations:

1834	Coorg
1843	Sindh
1849	Punjab
1852	Lower Burma
1853	Nagpur
1856	Oudh

In the meantime, the Company signed treaties of alliance and protection with numerous local sovereigns. As a result, the princes became vassals of the Company, retaining their prerogatives with regard to the administration and defence of their territory, but accepting scrutiny from a British resident.

The Maratha Wars

The Maratha Confederacy occupied large tracts of land in central India. The Maratha Army was recognised for its warlike qualities and, until 1775, the Company had refrained from intervening in the internal affairs of the Maratha state. In 1775, the usurper, Peshwa, Raghunath Rao, faced opposition from local lords who supported his rival. He managed to obtain the support of the British in exchange for territorial and financial concessions. The Anglo-Indian Army was first held in check at Talegaon in January 1779. The Governor-General, Warren Hastings, did everything he could to redress the situation. In 1780, Company troops occupied Ahmedabad and Bassein. Then, in 1781, the Maratha forces led by Mahadji Sindhia were defeated at Sipri. The Treaty of Salbai brought the war to an end and gave the Company the right to keep an eye on Maratha affairs.

In 1803, the Maratha leaders took steps to free themselves from the Company's hold. Governor-General Wellesley decided to attack them on two fronts: his brother, Arthur Wellesley, directed operations in Deccan and totally defeated the Maratha army at Assaye. In the north, General Lake routed the Sindhia's army at Delhi and Laswaree. This British offensive would give the Company ten years' respite.

In 1813, the new Governor-General, Lord Hastings, adopted an interventionist and omnipresent policy toward the Peshwa. Exasperated, the Maratha ransacked and burned the British residence in Poona. The 28,000-strong Maratha army encountered the Company's army of fewer than 3,000 men at Khirkee. The Maratha defeat was total.

In 1818, the position of Peshwa was abolished and Poona's lands were annexed to the Presidency of Bombay, marking the end of the Maratha Confederacy.

The Sikh Wars

In 1845, the Company adopted a provocative attitude towards the Sikh kingdom, gathering 35,000 men at the border and building bridges across the Sutlej River that protected Lahore. In December, the Sikhs decided to take the initiative and attacked the British army.

The Company's troops achieved their first success at Maudkee, with a second battle taking place at Ferozeshah where the Sikhs lost 8,000 men against 2,000 of their opponents. The British also won at Aliwar. These successes were crowned by the victory at Sobraon which put an end to the war in February 1846. The Treaty of Lahore imposed strict limitations on the Sikh army and granted the Company significant territorial advantages in the Punjab.

In 1848, humiliated by the Treaty of Lahore, the Sikhs rose again. Led by General Gough, a powerful Anglo-Indian Army defeated the Sikhs successively in Chillianwallah and Multan and finally in Gujarat. By March 1849, the war was over and the Sikh kingdom had been annihilated and their lands were broken up. A Dogra Prince, who supported the British, was granted Kashmir. Other parts of the kingdom were added to the Company's territorial possessions.

The Sikhs would become loyal allies of the Company. Their loyalty remained firm throughout the Burmese Wars and the repression of the Mutiny in 1857.

1.4 Peacemaking

The Company's army was called on to intervene several times – not to undertake territorial conquests, but to put down uncontrolled elements threatening internal security. These expeditions often took the form of genuine campaigns, mobilising large numbers of troops.

The Rohillas (1774 and 1794)

The Rohillas were Afghan tribes who, in the past, had obtained the right to settle in India and found a quasi-independent state there: Rohilkund. Preserving their ancestral traditions, the Rohillas happily sacked and pillaged wherever they went, wreaking havoc on the surrounding areas.

In 1774, Warren Hastings led the first expedition against them. Twenty years later, it took a second war to defeat the Rohillas once and for all.

The Pindaris (1816-1818)

The Pindaris were local armed groups, often led by feudal warlords who rampaged through central India. The leaders of the Maratha Confederacy frequently used them as auxiliary troops which gave them a certain degree of impunity.

In 1816, after its victory over the Maratha, the Company took the decision to wipe out the Pindaris. It took an army in excess of 100,000 men, supported by 300 cannon, to do the job. Pushing the Pindaris back, the Anglo-Indian Army gradually reduced their number until, by 1818, they had been totally exterminated.

The Pirates (1819-1821)

The Persian Gulf was infested with pirates. Based on the Arabian Peninsula, these pirates were threatening lines of communication while also carrying out incursions along the Indian coasts. The Bombay army was called on to deal with them.

The 3rd and 5th Bombay Light Infantry disembarked in 1819, but were attacked by the Beni Boo Ali tribe which inflicted heavy losses on them. In 1821, a new expedition put an end to the Beni Boo Ali with 200 killed, 150 of whom came from the 13th Bombay Infantry.

The North West Frontier

As soon as the Company took control of the Punjab, one of its main concerns was securing the north west frontier. This mountainous region experienced conflict throughout all the years of British domination. Special units were created to deal with the problem, the Guides and the Punjab Irregular Force. Their job was to respond effectively to the specific conditions of a war consisting of raids and skirmishes led by the warlike tribes of the region and by Afghan incursions.

Beyond these local struggles, the north west frontier with Afghanistan took on considerable strategic importance when it became clear that it was a natural line of defence against any Russian aspiration towards India. Right up until the Second World War, the Northwest frontier remained a trouble hotspot and a battle training ground for Indian units.

1.5 The Mutiny of the Bengal Army

Proud of its successes and puffed up with pride from its conquests, the Company's army would face a crisis in 1857 that was so serious that it could have threatened the British presence in India. By 1850, relations between British officers and their Indian troops in the Bengal Army had deteriorated. Army officers were living in a world of their own, far from the concerns of their men. The relative peace that followed the various conquests had not improved these relations, either. The distant and haughty attitude of the British, combined with poor military management, foreshadowed future difficulties.

In 1857, mutiny broke out among a large part of the Bengal army. It came like a clap of thunder: 64 regiments mutinied or had to be disarmed. The trigger for the mutiny was the "cartridges affair", even though signs of discontent had been simmering well beforehand.

"The cartridges affair"

In 1856, native troops were equipped with the breech-loading Enfield rifle. Loading this rifle required tearing open the cartridge with one's teeth. A rumour claimed that the cartridges were coated with a layer of cow and pig fat – which was good reason for Hindus and Muslims alike not to use them.

In 1857, 57 soldiers from the 3rd Bengal Light Cavalry were sentenced to heavy penalties for refusing to use the cartridges. On 10 May, the three regiments in the town of Meerut mutinied. Massacring their officers and any European they came across, they set their comrades free and stirred up the local people. Marching on Delhi, they restored the Mughal Bahadur II to the throne. He had been living there, secluded, for several years. The uprising spread quickly and soon reached the cities of Benares, Allahabad, Cawnpore and Lucknow.

Cawnpore was to become the symbol of recapture for the British – and the justification for ferocious repression. The garrison at Cawnpore, which had been under siege for several weeks, obtained permission from the mutineers to leave the besieged camp. Three hundred Europeans, including women and children, were part of the retreat. The terms of the agreement had been approved by Nana Sahib, a descendant of the Maratha Peshwas. While boarding the boats that were supposed to take them to a safe place, the British were caught in crossfire, killing all but four of the men. Women and children were locked up by the rebels and massacred a few days later by the local people.

In order to quell the rebellion, the British called on the Company's European troops and the Punjabi regiments. The British decisiveness and organisation quickly restored the initiative to the Anglo-Indian troops.

On 10 June, the British laid siege to Delhi, which they took on 20th September. Repression was fierce and thousands of Indians were executed. Shortly thereafter, reinforcements arrived from Britain and the Company was ready to embark on the reconquest of the lost territories. An amnesty was offered to the rebels, many of whom surrendered. The victory at Gwalior (19 June 1858) put a final end to the military threat from the mutineers. However, resistance in Oudh was not finally snuffed out until April 1859.

The mutiny, marked by merciless ferocity on both sides, had lasted two years. Britain learned its lesson from the events and India was placed under the direct control of the Crown. At the same time, a more flexible policy was implemented towards the Indian leaders. The army was purged and many rebel – or suspected rebel – units disappeared.

2

The Army of the Crown

2.1 The end of the century: organisation

The Indian mutiny of 1857 caused the Indian Acts, which transferred control of India from the Company to the British government in 1858. This was the time when the Hindi term "Raj", meaning "rule", came to prominence. The European troops of the Company were directly integrated into the British army. Indian regiments of the three presidencies protected their identity and stayed under command of their previous leaders.

All the remaining units of the Bengal army which had escaped disbandment were re-numbered. There were no changes in the army of Madras. In the Bombay's army, where only two regiments had mutinied, the vacant numbers were filled by the raising of new units. In order to reduce possible risks of mutiny, "classes"[1] were mixed into the regiments. The new structure only allowed homogeneity at company or squadron level.

After the second Afghan War of 1880, a few regiments were disbanded. For reasons of economy, the high command thought they were no longer needed. A few years later, the Anglo-Russian crisis raised fears of war on the north west frontier. The disbanded regiments were recalled and reconstituted. New regiments were also raised. During the same period, the term "native", considered pejorative, was abandoned.

The restructuring of the presidency armies was the subject of many reports produced by various committees and commissions. The merging of the armies of Bengal, Bombay and Madras was decided by the Eden Committee of 1878 but was only effective in 1895. From then on, the Commander-in-chief had authority on four regional commands:

Bengal: headquarters in Niani Tal;
Bombay: headquarters in Poona, controlling Sind, Baluchistan and Aden;
Madras: headquarters in Ootacamund, controlling Burma and Hyderabad;
Punjab: headquarters in Murree, controlling the Frontier Force.

	BENGAL	PUNJAB	MADRAS	BOMBAY	HYDERABAD
Cavalry regiments	19	5	3	7	4
Infantry battalions	41	10	19	23	5
Gurkhas battalions	14	-	-	-	-
Artillery batteries	4	5	-	1	4
Sapper companies	1	-	1	1	-

When the Boer War broke out in South-Africa (1899-1902), the British battalions were replaced by Indian units in a few colonial garrisons:

In Burma	6 infantry battalions and 2 Gurkha battalions
In Ceylon	1 infantry battalion
In China	5 infantry battalions
In Hong-Kong	1 infantry battalion
In Mauritius	2 infantry battalions
In Singapore	2 infantry battalions
In Aden	1 infantry battalion

---

1   Classes or religions

Field Marshal, 1930. (Artwork by Mike Chappell)

2.2 Operations

Throughout the period 1856-1914, the Indian Army was almost continuously in action.

On the North West Frontier

1859-1860	Expedition against the Mahsuds following the murder of a British officer.
1863	Expedition against the Yusufzai.
1877-1878	Expedition against the Afridis who threatened the Kohat-Peshawar road.
1884	Expedition in the Zhob Valley.
1888	Expedition against the Hazaras (Black Mountain).
1891	Expedition along the Afghan border on the Samana Ridge.
1891	Expedition in the Black Mountain region.
1894-1895	New campaign against the Mahsuds.
1895	Defence and relief of Chitral.
1897-1898	General uprising on the Frontier. 36,000 troops were needed to suppress the revolt.
1901-1902	Campaign against the Waziris.
1908	Expedition against the Mohmands.

On the North East Frontier

1864-1866	Punitive expedition in Bhutan.
1871-1872	Expedition against the Lushai tribe.
1879-1880	Expedition against the Nagas.
1888	Campaign in Sikkin.
1887-1894	Conquest of Upper Burma.
1904	Campaign in Tibet.
1911-1912	Expedition against the Abor tribe in Assam.

Overseas service

The two main tasks of the Indian Army were domestic security and defence of frontiers. Nevertheless, the size of the army did not give Britain a valuable tool to intervene where needed. Indian soldiers played a significant role in the following campaigns:

China	1856-1860	Seizure of the Taku Forts and occupation of Peking.
Persia:	1856-1857	Securing frontier with Persia.
Abyssinia:	1868	Destruction of King Theodore's capital.
Malaya:	1874-1876	Operation in Perak.
Afghanistan	1878-1880	Secure Afghanistan against Russian influence.
Malta:	1878	7,000 Indian troops sent to counter a possible Russian action against Turkey.
Egypt:	1882	Protection of Suez Canal.
Sudan:	1885	Operations against tribes.
Sudan:	1896-1898	Reconquest of Sudan.
East Africa	1896-1900	Several small actions against coastal tribes.
Central Africa	1894-1898	Punitive expeditions in the Great Lakes region.
China:	1900	Suppression of the Boxer Rebellion and occupation of Peking.
Somaliland	1901-1910	Three campaigns against the "Mad Mullah".

2.2.1 Kitchener's reforms (1903-1910)

Viscount Kitchener of Khartoum was appointed Commander-in-Chief of the Indian Army in 1903. Over the next seven years, he put into effect a wide range of reforms which were about to transform the Indian Army into an efficient 20th century army force.

The first reform consisted in renumbering the army's regiments. The three presidency armies had been unified in 1895, but each regiment had continued to retain both its old number and the name of the presidency which had raised it. Kitchener abolished these numbers and titles and re-numbered all regiments in sequence.

Kitchener then considered the Indian Staff Corps. After 1857, many British officers had been detached from their regiments to fill civilian posts. In order to replace them, officers were no longer posted directly to a regiment, instead they joined the Staff Corps and were only attached to the regiment in which they served. By the end of the 19th century, the development of the Indian Civil Corps had allowed many officers to return to their unit. The Staff Corps was no longer required, it was abolished and officers were once again fully part of their regiment.

Kitchener also abandoned the policy of distributing the army around the country, mainly for internal security purposes, and of rarely moving regiments outside their own area. Regiments were made liable for service anywhere in India and all were required to provide duty time on the North West Frontier in order to gain field experience.

ARMY OF THE NORTH	ARMY OF THE SOUTH
1st Peshawar Division	4th Quetta Division
2nd Rawalpindi Division	5th Mow Division
3rd Lahore Division	6th Poona Division
7th Meerut Division	9th Secunderabad Division
8th Lucknow Division	Burman Division
Bannu Brigade	Aden Brigade
Derajat Brigade	
Kohat Brigade	

Higher formations (brigades, divisions and armies) were established in peace time to be immediately operational, if necessary.

The build-up of large formations created the need for more qualified staff officers. As it was difficult and expensive to send Indian Army officers to attend the Staff College in England, Kitchener founded the Indian Staff College at Quetta.

It should be remembered that the Army in India was a mixed force of British and Indian units.

The British Army in India was made up of:

9 cavalry regiments

52 infantry battalions

11 Royal Horse Artillery batteries

45 Royal Field Artillery batteries

20 mountain artillery batteries

21 Garrison Artillery companies

1 Engineering company

The Indian Army was composed of:

39 cavalry regiments

138 infantry battalions

12 mountain batteries

1 garrison battery

19 companies of Sappers & Miners

4 signal companies

2 railway companies

All troops in India were under the single command of a commander-in-chief assisted by a chief of staff. The most important positions were held alternatively by officers of the British and Indian armies. When the commander-in-chief was from the Indian army, the chief-of-staff was from the British army, and vice-versa. The alternation was also valid at other levels of the hierarchy.

2.2.2 The First World War

At the beginning of the First World War, the Indian Army was the only organised force of the Commonwealth apart from the British Army. It was 77,000 Europeans and 160,000 Indian troops strong, most of them under the command of British officers. The Indian Army fought in most theatres of war with devotion to duty.

The government of India immediately offered two cavalry and two infantry divisions for service overseas. This Corps, designated as "Expeditionary Force A" was originally intended to relieve British troops in Egypt, but was quickly diverted to the Western Front. They arrived just in time to participate in the Battle of la Bassée (October 1914).

In March 1915, 7th (Meerut) Division led the assault during the battle of Neuve-Chapelle.

The two infantry divisions left France in October 1915. The cavalry divisions fought in France until 1918. In the spring of 1918, they sailed to Egypt to be integrated into the Desert Mounted Corps of the "E Force". The largest Indian force was "Expeditionary Force D" which was sent to Mesopotamia, mainly to protect British oil installations. It was quickly reinforced and more and more involved in mainland operations targeting Baghdad. Force D encountered a major unexpected resistance from the Turks, leading to the Kut disaster during which the 6th Poona Division was forced to capitulate. Later, in the same theatre, British and Indian troops gained the initiative and ended the war with victories in Palestine and with the seizure of Baghdad. Between 1914 and 1919, about one million Indians served outside their country at the cost of 60,000 soldiers killed and 70,000 wounded.

The war had clearly revealed the logistic weaknesses of the Indian Army. The replacement and reinforcement systems, the supply of food and equipment had been left so much to regimental initiative that it had proven ineffective. The end of the war called for military reforms.

Indian Expeditionary Forces 1914-1919

Force "A" France & Flanders	1st Cavalry Division 2nd Cavalry Division 3rd (Lahore) Infantry Division 7th (Meerut) Infantry Division	1914-1918 1914-1918 1914-1915 1914-1915
Force "B" East Africa	27th (Bengalore) Brigade of 9th Division Imperial Service Brigade	1914
Force "C" Ouganda	29th Punjabis ISF, Contingents from: Bharatpur, Jind, Kapurthala, Rampore	1915-1918
Force "D" Mesopotamia & Palestine	Cavalry Division (created from the 6th, 7th and 11th independent brigades) 6th (Poona) Infantry Division 3rd and 7th (Meerut) Infantry Division 12th, 14th 15th, 17th and 18th Infantry Division	1916-1918 1914-1916 1915-1918
Force "E" Egypt (1918)	1st Mounted Division (4th Cavalry Division) 2nd Mounted Division (5th Cavalry Division) 11th Infantry Division	
Force "F" Egypt (1915)	28th, 29th and 30th Brigade of 10th Division	
Force "G" Gallipoli (1916)	29th Brigade of 10th Infantry Division (detached)	
` Captured at Kut by the Turks		

2.2.3 The interwar period

In March 1919, taking advantage of the weakness of the Indian Army still present in the country, the Afghan forces invaded the Western Frontier and seized several cities. Only two regular cavalry regiments and eight regular infantry battalions were able to react fast. The other available units were part of the Indian Territorial Force (ITF). British and Indian units were quickly mobilised and a British attack, supported by the Air Force, rapidly defeated the invaders. Cease fire was concluded by the end of the month.

As expected, an important reorganisation was decided in 1922:

Infantry battalions were amalgamated in larger regiments;

The number of cavalry regiments was reduced due to the new requirements of modern warfare;

Full dress was replaced by khaki for every occasion.

As for infantry units, the 131 regular battalions were merged to form 20 large regiments, each with a 10th battalion serving as a permanent depot and training centre. The 1922 reorganisation also created a territorial army similar to the one known in Europe. The numbering of territorial battalions started with no. 11.

By grouping them in pairs, the cavalry regiments were reduced from 39 to 20. Only the 27th and 28th regiments and the Guides Cavalry remained unchanged.

Generals, 1916 and 1945. (Artwork by Mike Chappell)

Indian Infantry Divisions in the Second World War.

The first exception to khaki dress uniform was noted in the 1925 Dress Regulations where mess dress was approved and allowed in regimental colours.[2] The Body Guards, however, had kept their superb uniforms in order to compensatefor the brightness of the local Princes and their escorts. Authorisation to wear full dress was then extended to officers attending levées and special functions or occasions. The ceremony of the 1937 Coronation gave the London crowd an opportunity to admire, once again, the splendid uniforms of the Indian Army.

During the interwar period, the army was organised to fulfil different missions.

The Field Army with a strength of four infantry divisions and eight cavalry brigades. A covering force of 12 infantry brigades and supporting arms had the task of securing the borders and act as a screening force in case of invasion.

The Internal Security Troops, made up of 43 battalions, were allotted the role of assisting the civil power in case of disturbances. If necessary, they could be backed up by field army units.

---

2   Carman, Indian Army Uniforms.

By the outbreak of the Second World War, as many as one third of the Indian Army were on internal security duties.[3]

In 1936, the Fakir of Ipi led 20,000 Pathan warriors against the British. Attacking from the Malakand, they threatened the British presence in Peshawar. Massive use of artillery and bombing by the Air Force ended the invasion that was motivated by religious fanaticism. To illustrate the ferocity of the battles, it must be mentioned that during this short campaign 1,000 Anglo-Indian soldiers lost their lives.

2.2.4 The Second World War

Despite important contributions from other Commonwealth and colonial forces, the British would never have won its campaigns in East Africa, North Africa and Western Asia without the Indian Army.

In October 1939, the Indian Army (including State Forces and Gurkhas, but excluding British units) had 189,000 men in its ranks:

> 133 infantry battalions
> 22 armoured and cavalry regiments
> 4 field artillery batteries
> 28 construction companies

In August 1945, at the peak of its strength, the Indian Army consisted of 2,640,000 soldiers and officers in:

> 268 infantry battalions,
> 19 armoured and cavalry regiments,
> 207 artillery batteries, and
> 107 construction companies.

When the Second World War broke out, no single unit of the Indian Army was motorised to acceptable standards. The troops were not prepared and trained at all for the type of warfare they were going to be faced with. Pre-war plans called for India to contribute limited forces to the defence of British interests in the Near East and Egypt.

Given the succession of crises in the Middle Eastern theatre, and the perception of western Asia as a gateway to the Indian subcontinent, the British command diverted brigade after brigade of the Indian Army to campaign in and garrison the Western Desert, Italian East Africa, Iraq, Persia, the Levant and Cyprus. The Indian troops were of mixed quality, ranging from the excellent 3rd and 4th Indian Divisions to the less well-trained, equipped and experienced battalions which whiled away the war in the dusty garrisons of Persia and Iraq.

As Indian brigades were often transferred among divisions and as battalions were often interchanged among brigades, the whole story of Second World War units is difficult to track.

As much as practicable, Indian brigades included a pair of Indian battalions and a single British battalion. Divisional artillery, supporting arms and services tended to be provided from the British army. But, as the war went on, more of these came from Indian assets. In the Burma theatre, General Slim preferred to segregate British and Indian battalions into their own brigades, believing that each fought better under that organisation.

In Africa and Italy, 4th, 5th, 8th and 10th divisions distinguished themselves in hard fought campaigns, taking an important part in the victories of Sidi-el-Barrani (December 1940), Alam-el-Alfa (September 1942) and El Alamein (November 1942). The Indian troops serving in Italy added the names of the Sangro River (November 1943), Cassino (March 1944) and the Gothic line (September 1944) to their glory.

In Asia, nothing had been foreseen to protect Malaya and Burma. The Japanese invasion quickly brought the war to India's doorstep. British and Indian troops were thrown out of Malaya, Hong-Kong, Singapore and Burma. The army trained intensively for jungle warfare and improved its supplies and equipment. Lines of communications were also improved.

In 1943, General Slim claimed that the Indian divisions of the 14th Army were among the best in the world. The reconquest of Burma was one of the most difficult campaigns of the war. The "Invade India" army of Japan was broken up and defeated.

---

3   Sumner, The Indian Army 1914-1947, Osprey.

By the end of the war, the Indian Army, at the cost of more than 100,000 casualties, had won 31 Victoria Crosses and more than 4,000 different awards. There is no better testimony of their value and sacrifice. The officers and men displayed the highest level of motivation and gallantry on the battlefield.

	THEATRE OF OPERATIONS: ASIA
Assam	20th and 21st Infantry Division
Burma	3rd (Chindit) 5th, 7th, 14th, 17th, 19th, 20th, 23rd, 25th, 26th Infantry Divisions, 44th Airborne Division 1st Burmese Division (destroyed in May 1942)
Ceylon	34th Infantry Division
Indochina	20th Infantry Division
Java	5th, 23rd and 26th Infantry Division
Malaya	9th and 11th Infantry Division (both captured in 1942) in Singapore 7th, 23rd and 25th Infantry Division
Sumatra	26th Infantry Division
	THEATRE OF OPERATIONS: NORTH AFRICA, EUROPE, MIDDLE EAST
Western Egypt and Desert	5th, 8th and 10th Infantry Division – 31st Armoured Division
Eritrea	4th and 5th Infantry Division
Greece	4th Infantry Division
Iraq	2nd, 6th, 10th and 12th Infantry Division – 31st Armoured Division
Iran	3rd, 10th and 12th Infantry Division
Italy	4th, 8th and 10th Infantry Division, 43rd Independent Brigade
Sudan	5th Infantry Division
Syria	4th and 8th Infantry Division – 31st Armoured Division
Tunisia	4th Infantry Division

2.2.5 Independence and Partition (1947)

By the end of the war, Indian troops were still engaged overseas. Many units served as occupation troops and were also responsible for maintaining law and order in recently liberated territories. Their task in Indonesia in support of the Dutch colonial troops became particularly difficult. 49th Brigade, detached from 23rd Division, lost 18 officers and 374 men within three days of combat against nationalist rebels. It was deemed necessary to reinforce the Indian troops with the full 5th Division, supported by armoured elements in order to control the main urban centres.

In August 1947, the British government agreed to transfer the power to Indians and to give independence to India. The territory was to be divided to allow the Muslim minority to enjoy its own state.

All Indian troops went back to the motherland. The partition of the Raj into two states led to the division of the army between the Indian Republic and Pakistan. About two thirds of the units went to India and one third was attributed to Pakistan. The partition of the Indian Army was completed with the discipline and professionalism that defined the army of the Raj, contrasting with the savage disorder devastating large portions of the territory. Brothers-in-arms left each to their new army, not knowing that within a year they would be enemies.

Four out of the Army's ten Gurkha regiments were transferred to the British Army forming the Gurkha brigade. The six remaining regiments went to the Indian Army.

The army of the Raj has disappeared but it will, for a long time, leave a lasting imprint on the traditions, uniforms and habits of the regiments of India and Pakistan.

PART II

The regiments of the Indian Army

To be able to shape a soul and establish traditions, any army needs to experience warfare and, in this regard, the Indian Army was not left out. Indeed, the history of the Indian Army is studded with a long series of campaigns aiming at either consolidating Britain's dominion over the country, or at taking part in conflicts involving colonial power.

In spite of a number of uproars and rebellions that marked three centuries of coexistence between the European corps of officers and their native troops, a special bond was forged between the Indian soldiers and their officers. The context behind this bond is the regiment. Whether a sepoy or a sowar, the Indian soldier devoted his whole life, his honour and his word (izzat), to the regiment he joined. This feeling was further reinforced by the environment in which the soldiers lived – as part of the company or squadron, surrounded by men of the same "class" and sharing the same values.

As for British officers, they soon gave an elitist and sportsmanship character to their service in India. After the Mutiny of 1857, however, officers paid increasing attention to the psychology and special features of their troops. The best officers of the British army took immense pride in serving in India. From father to son, generations of officers became attached to their men and their regiment.

3

The Cavalry

Members of the Indian Cavalry were generally recruited from well-to-do classes, using methods inherited from the Company. Except for 26th, 27th and 28th Light Cavalry, which were formed from the Madras regular cavalry, the *Silladar* system prevailed. This system meant that every cavalryman had to supply his own horse, equipment and uniform, with the Government providing only his weapons. During the First World War, the *Silladar* system demonstrated its limitations. For units engaged overseas, there was no question of replacing horses and equipment on an individual basis, so the regiment stepped in and provided both in return for a sum of money (*assami*), that the soldier would recover at the end of his active service. However, this initiative, which was taken at a regimental level, soon lead to anarchy, with each regiment trying to make itself as conspicuous as possible.

The *Silladar* system was gradually abandoned because it no longer met the requirements of a modern army. The Indian cavalry regiment was divided into four squadrons, each consisting of two troops – that is about 600 officers and men.

After the First World War, the cavalry were far more numerous than needed in modern war, and their number was halved by the amalgamation of pairs of almost all regiments. Three regiments – the 27th and 28th (the oldest in the army) and the Guides Cavalry – remained unchanged.

The new cavalry regiments were grouped around seven permanent regimental centres with regiments taking turns as the recruiting and training unit for the group. This system gave way in 1936 to three troops for the remaining eighteen regiments, with one regiment[1] in each group (12th Sam Browne's Cavalry, 15th Lancers and 20th Lancers) removed from active service and permanently assigned to the training role.

> 1st group (Jhansi): regiments 1, 2, 3, 16, 17, 18 and 15 (Training)
> 2nd group (Ferozepore): regiments 4, 5, 10, 11, 13, 14 and 12 (Training)
> 3rd group (Lucknow): regiment 6, 7, 8, 9, 19, 21 and 20 (Training)

Mechanisation began in 1938 with 13th DCO Lancers and Scinde Horse swapping their horses for armoured cars. The last unit to complete the conversion was 19th KGO Lancers in 1940. The number of the regiment was given prominence in 1922 but, during the 1930s, many of these were turned into subtitles, giving prominence to better-known regimental names instead.

---

1   Training regiments were the 12th, 15th and 20th. All three were disbanded after the independence.

The Bodyguards

Lineage

The Governor-General's Bodyguard
The Governor's Bodyguard, Bombay
The Governor's Bodyguard, Madras
The Governor's Bodyguard, Bengal
Nepal Escort

The Bodyguards

The first bodyguard raised in India was composed of Europeans recruited in 1762 from the East India Company's Infantry. The troops, which became useless cavalry and expensive to maintain, were disbanded shortly afterwards.

In 1773, the Governor of Bengal raised a body of Indian cavalrymen. The official designation at this time was "The Governor's Troops of Moghuls". The corps was the only mounted unit of the Bengal forces until 1777.

The Bodyguards were not only ceremonial troops, they performed brilliantly during the early campaigns of the Company. They received their first battle honour (Java) for the seizure of Batavia in 1804. Other honours were awarded for their participation in the first Burma War and the Sikh Wars.

Recruitment to the corps varied over time: originally, transfer to the corps from other cavalry units was a reward for good service but the regiments were reluctant to let their best men go. The men were then directly enrolled for the whole of their service. The Bodyguard was composed of four squadrons: two Sikh squadrons and two Punjabi Muslim squadrons.

The Bodyguards of the Governors of Madras and Bombay were raised later for the protection of the Governors of these Presidencies. In Madras, the ranks were composed of Rajput and Jats and in Bombay of Ranghars[2] and Sikhs. In 1912, the Governor of Bengal formed his Bodyguard troop from volunteers of the Indian Cavalry regiments – mainly Punjabi Muslim and Rajput. The British resident in Nepal also benefitted with escort services provided by the Nepal Escort.

During the First World War, the Bodyguards were used as a remount and depot unit for cavalry serving overseas. The Bodyguards served in the Second World War in 44th Divisional Squadron (GGBG) of 2nd Indian Airborne Division. In 1946, they reverted to their original title.

Partition
The Bodyguard squadrons were divided between India and Pakistan.
Last dress uniform
Scarlet, blue facings.
Class composition (1940)
Sikhs, Punjabi Muslims.

Battle Honours
Java, Ava, Mahrajapore, Moodkee, Ferozeshah, Aliwal, Sobraon

---

2   (5) Ranghars : muslims from Rajputana.

Bodyguard 1930. (Artwork by Mike Chappell)

Skinner's Horse
(1st Duke of York's own Cavalry)

Lineage

1803	Captain Skinner's Corps of Irregular Horse
1815	3rd Regiment of Local Horse
1823	1st Regiment of Local Horse
1840	1st Bengal Irregular Cavalry
1861	1st Regiment of Bengal Cavalry
1861	3rd Regiment of Bengal Cavalry
1896	1st Regiment of Bengal Lancers
1899	1st (The Duke of York's Own) Regiment of Bengal Lancers
1901	1st (The Duke of York's Own) Bengal Lancers (Skinner's Horse)
1903	1st Duke of York's Own Lancers (Skinner's Horse)
1903	3rd Skinner's Horse

Skinner's Horse

1st DYO Cavalry were born from the fusion of 1st DYO Lancers with 3rd Skinner's Horse.

In 1803, the regular troops of the Mahratta princes were defeated by Lord Lake before Delhi. From then on, units decided to change their employers and offered their services to the British. They accepted to serve the British under two conditions: never fight against Scindia, and permission to choose their own leader.

One of these units was a cavalry *rissalah* which had been commanded by James Skinner, dismissed from his service after refusing to fight against the Company's army. The cavalry *rissalah* claimed him as their own. James Skinner set out to command the finest cavalry regiment in the service of John Company. After seizing Malaghur, the regiment surprised the Sikhs' leaders who were about to joint hands with the Holkar's army. The Skinner's chased Amir Khan away, 700 miles from his own territory.

In 1815, the Corps consisted of three units of 1,000 men each. Four years later, the 3rd was disbanded and Robert Skinner, James's younger brother, commanded the 2nd Regiment. The two regiments were brigaded for a time but, from 1818, each had a separate existence.

1st Corps participated in the capture of Bhurtpore and 2nd Corps played an important part in the Afghanistan campaign of 1839. 1st Regiment also marched into Afghanistan, earning an honour for the fight around Kandahar in 1842. 3rd Regiment of local Horse were involved in the First Sikh War. When revolt crept over the army of Bengal, the 1st were employed in putting down insurrection along the banks of the Ravi. The 2nd saw service in Oudh and Bundelkand. Both units were in Afghanistan (1879-1880). By the turn of the century, the Skinner's made brilliant charges, cutting up the Tartar Cavalry during the Chinese expedition.

In 1914, the 3rd proceeded to France with the Meerut Cavalry Brigade to take part in all the actions of 2nd Cavalry Division. The 1st remained on the North West Frontier. Both Corps saw action during the third Afghanistan conflict. The spring of 1921 found the regiments at Sialkot for amalgamation.

The unit was mechanised in 1939 and became the reconnaissance unit of 4th Indian Division. In 1941, the Skinner's fought in Italian East Africa. Back in Egypt, they were sent to Italy where they became the reconnaissance regiment of 10th Indian Division.

Partition
In 1947, the regiment is assigned to the Indian Army.
Last dress uniform
Canary yellow, black facings.
Class composition (1940)
Ranghars, Rajput, Jats, Hindustani Muslims.

Battle Honours
Bhurtpore, Ghunzee 1839, Afghanistan 1839; Khelat, Candahar 1842, Maharajpore, Moodkee, Ferozeshah, Aliwal, Kandahar 1880, Afghanistan 1879-80, Punjab Frontier, Pekin 1900, France and Flanders 1914-16, North West Frontier, India 1915, Baluchistan, Afghanistan 1919, Argodat, Keren, Amba Alagi, East Africa, Western Desert, Abyssinia 1940-41, Senio Floodbank, Italy 1943-45.

1st Skinner's Horse, 1912. (Artwork by Mike Chappell)

2nd Royal Lancers
(Gardner's Horse)

Lineage

1809	Gardner's Horse
1838	4th Cavalry
1840	6th Bengal Irregular Cavalry
1851	2nd Bengal Cavalry
1858	4th Bengal Cavalry
1890	2nd Regiment of Bengal Lancers
1900	4th Bengal Lancers
1903	2nd Lancers (Gardner's Horse)
1903	4th Lancers
1904	4th Cavalry

2nd Royal Lancers (Gardner's Horse)

The 2nd Lancers (Gardner's Horse) and 4th Cavalry formed 2nd Royal Lancers.

2nd Lancers   William Gardner, an officer of 74th Highlanders had left the Queen's service for a career with the Mahratta army. In 1809, after refusing to proceed against the British, he joined the Company's forces and raised the Corps which now bears his name. Gardner's Regiment was first engaged in the Nepal war in 1815 and earned great fame in Burma where they gained the exclusive honour "Arracan". Subsequently, 2nd Lancers served in Egypt and on the North West Frontier.

4th Lancers   have their origin in a cavalry regiment raised in 1838 for service with the King of Oudh. In 1840, they were transferred back to the Bengal Army and saw active service on the North West Frontier in Baluchistan and in the second Afghan War.

In 1914, 2nd Lancers was part of the Cavalry Corps who served in France for three years. The 4th proceeded to France as the Meerut Division Cavalry and followed the division to Egypt. The amalgamation of both regiments took place in Bombay in April 1923.

In 1939, the Gardner's Horse fought in Egypt with the 3rd Motorised Brigade. Twice decimated and twice reconstituted, the regiment participated in the North African Campaign before returning to India in 1943, where it served on the North West Frontier.

Partition
On partition, the regiment was allocated to India.
Last dress uniform
Blue, light blue facings.
Class composition (1940)
Ranghars, Rajput, Jats, Hindustani Muslims.

Battle Honours
Arracan, Sobraon, Punjaub, Mooltan 1857-58, Afghanistan 1879-80, Tel-el-Kebir, Egypt 1882, La Bassee 1914, Givenchy 1914, Neuve Chapelle, Festubert 1915, Somme 1916, Morval, Cambrai 1917, France and Flanders 1914-18, Egypt 1915, Megiddo, Sharon, Damascus, Palestine 1918, Tigris 1916, Mesopotamia 1915-16, Afghanistan 1919, El Mechili, Point 171.

2nd Gardner's Horse, 1902 and 1930. (Artwork by Mike Chappell)

3rd Cavalry

Lineage

1841	7th Bengal Irregular Cavalry
1846	18th Bengal Irregular Cavalry
1861	5th Bengal Cavalry
1861	8th Bengal Cavalry
1890	8th Bengal Lancers
1903	5th Cavalry
1903	8th Lancers
1906	8th Cavalry

3rd Cavalry

3rd Cavalry results from the amalgamation of two old irregular cavalry regiments of the Company's Bengal army: **5th** and **8th**.

5th Cavalry was raised in Bareilly in 1841 as a consequence of the Afghan War. It participated in the Sikh War where it sometimes fought dismounted. After the second Afghan War, the 5th garrisoned on the North West Frontier.

In 1914, it was kept in India for internal security duties and went later to Mesopotamia to put down the Arab rebellion.

8th Cavalry was the last regiment to be raised before the Mutiny. It was given a new number in 1861 because ten regiments were disbanded following their participation in the Mutiny. The regiment was involved in the second Afghan War and it stayed in India during the First World War. The two corps were merged in Bombay in 1921. 3rd Cavalry were captured in Singapore by the Japanese in 1942. It was reconstituted in 1946 to become an airborne reconnaissance unit.

Partition
The regiment went to the Indian Army in 1947.
Last dress uniform
Blue, primrose facings.
Class composition (1940)
Ranghars, Rajput, Jats, Hindustani Muslims.

Battle Honours
Mooltan, Punjaub, Afghanistan 1878-80, Mesopotamia 1917-18, North Malaya, Central Malaya, Malaya 1941-42.

3rd Cavalry, 1906 and 1914. (Artwork by Mike Chappell)

Hodson's Horse
(4th Duke of Cambridge's Own Lancers)

Lineage

1857	Hodson's Horse
1858	1st Hodson's Horse
1858	2nd Hodson's Horse
1861	9th Bengal Cavalry
1861	10th Bengal Cavalry
1871	10th Bengal Lancers
1878	10th Bengal (Duke of Cambridge's Own)
1885	9th Bengal Lancers
1901	9th Bengal Lancers (Hodson's Horse)
1901	10th Duke of Cambridge's Own Bengal Lancers (Hodson Horse)
1903	9th Hodson's Horse
1903	10th Duke of Cambridge's Own Lancers (Hodson's Horse)

Hodson's Horse

The regiment was created by amalgamation of **9th Hodson's Horse** and **10th DCO Lancers.**

In 1857, William Hodson, then an officer of Bengal Fusiliers, raised *rissalahs* of Punjab cavalrymen who were mainly attracted by the possibilities of plundering the rich cities of Bengal. The corps played an important part in the Siege of Delhi where they captured the Moghul. Hodson won renown for the execution of the Moghul's sons.

The influx of recruits required the creation of three regiments. The junior unit was disbanded in 1860, and the men going over to Fane's Horse were formed for service in China. The two remaining units were re-numbered 9th and 10th Bengal Cavalry.

In 1867, the 10th went to Abyssinia and, in 1885, the 9th was the only Indian Cavalry regiment to participate in the Sudan campaign. In 1895, the 9th was employed by detachments in mountain warfare in Chitral. At the outbreak of the First World War, the 9th formed part of the Ambala Cavalry Brigade which fought in France and in the Middle East. The 10th distinguished itself in Mesopotamia and was part of the force which entered Baghdad.

The two corps were amalgamated in 1921 in Multan. During the Second World War, the regiment served in Egypt and Syria. They returned to India with four years' overseas service and not a single battle honour.

Partition
Hodson's Horse was allotted to India.
Last dress uniform
Blue, red facings.
Class composition (1940)
Dogras, Punjabi Muslims, Sikhs.

Battle Honours
Delhi 1857, Lucknow, Abyssinia, Afghanistan 1878-80, Suakin 1885, Chitral, Punjab Frontier, Givenchy 1914, Somme 1916, Bazentin, Flers-Courcelettes, Cambrai 1917, France & Flanders 1914-18, Megiddo, Sharon, Damascus, Palestine 1918, Khan Baghdadi, Mesopotamia 1916-18.

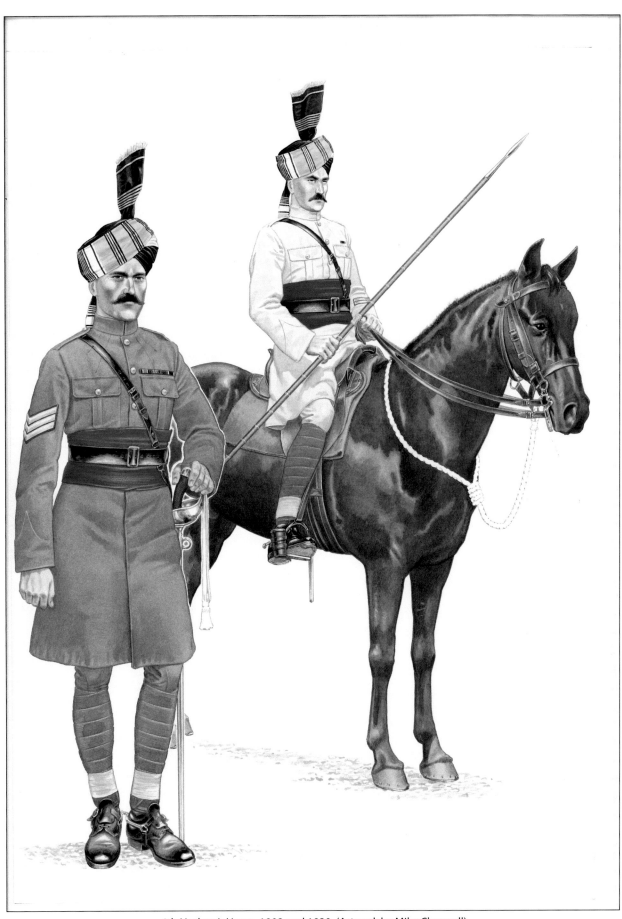

4th Hodson's Horse, 1902 and 1930. (Artwork by Mike Chappell)

Probyn's Horse
(5th King Edward VII's Own Lancers)

Lineage

1857	Wales' Horse
1857	2nd Sikh Irregular Cavalry
1857	1st Sikh Irregular Cavalry (Wales's Horse)
1860	1st Sikh Irregular Cavalry (Probyn's Horse)
1861	11th Bengal Cavalry
1861	12th Bengal Cavalry
1864	11th Bengal Cavalry (Lancers)
1864	11th Bengal Lancers
1876	11th Prince of Wales's Own Bengal Lancers
1903	12th Cavalry
1904	11th Prince of Wales's Own Bengal Lancers (Probyn's Horse)

Probyn's Horse (5th King Edward VII's Own Lancers)

The 5th Lancers is born from the amalgamation of **11th PWO Lancers** and **12th Cavalry.**

The two regiments were raised at Lahore in 1857 in order to fight the mutineers. Their original names were 1st and 2nd Sikh Irregular Cavalry. When the commanding officer of the 1st was killed, Major Dighton Probyn took over the command. In 1859, 1st Sikh participated in the China expedition. In 1868, the regiment's names were changed to 11th and 12th Bengal Cavalry, respectively. 12th Cavalry was present in Abyssinia. Both corps participated in the second Afghan War.

11th was engaged in the Black Mountain expedition and was part of the Malakand Field Force. During the First World War, both regiments saw action in the Middle East theatre.

Amalgamation took place in 1921. In the course of World War Two, 5th Lancers was first integrated in 1st Armoured Brigade and later in 255th Tank Brigade assuming an important role in the reconquest of Burma.

Partition
The regiment was integrated into the Pakistan army.
Last dress uniform
Blue, red facings.
Class composition (1940)
Dogras, Punjabi Muslims, Sikhs.

Battle Honours
Lucknow, Taku Forts, Pekin 1860, Abyssinia, All Masjid, Peiwar Kotal, Charasiah, Kabul 1879, Afghanistan 1878-80, Chitral, Malakand, Punjab Frontier, Mesopotamia 1915-18, Meiktila, Capture of Meiktila, Defence of Meiktila, Taungtha, Rangoon Road, Pyawbwe, Pyinmana, Toungoo, Pegu 1945, Burma 1942-45.

5th Probyn's Horse, 1890 and 1945. (Artwork by Mike Chappell)

6th Duke of Connaught's Own Lancers
(Watson's Horse)

Lineage

1857	Rohilkhand Horse
1858	4th Regiment of Sikh Irregular Cavalry
1861	13th Regiment of Bengal Cavalry
1862	16th Bengal Cavalry
1864	13th Regiment of Bengal Cavalry (Lancers)
1874	13th Regiment of Bengal Lancers
1884	13th Duke of Connaught's Regiment of Bengal Lancers
1885	16th Regiment of Bengal Cavalry
1900	16th Regiment of Bengal Lancers
1901	16th Bengal Lancers
1903	13th Duke of Connaught's Lancers
1903	16th Cavalry
1906	13th Duke of Connaught's Lancers (Watson's Horse)

6th Duke of Connaught's Own Lancers (Watson's Horse)

The two regiments which formed 6th Lancers were **13th DCO Lancers** and **16th Cavalry.** 4th Sikh Irregular Cavalry were raised in Lahore in 1858. The regiment was engaged in chasing the rebel leaders and captured Tantia Topi, one of the Mutiny's chiefs who had directed the Cawnpore massacre. In 1863, 4th Sikh became 13th Bengal Cavalry. They sailed to Egypt in 1882 to participate in the Tel-el-Kebir battle and harass Arabi Pasha into surrender. It was in Cairo that the Duke of Connaught's name was added to the regimental title.

In August 1897, two squadrons charged the Mohmands who besieged the Shabkadir Fort. During the Great War, the 13th was part of 7th Cavalry Brigade in Mesopotamia and delivered two outstanding cavalry charges; the first against the trenches of Tikrat, the second against a Turkish convoy close to Mosul.

16th Cavalry was first known as "Rohilkhand Horse". Raised in 1857, it was disbanded in 1882 for economic reasons. Three years later, it went back into service. The regiment saw action in China during the Boxers' uprising. In 1915, 16th joined IEF (D) in Mesopotamia, where it captured a Turkish standard at Shaiba.

The two regiments were amalgamated in Kohat in June 1921. In April 1942, 6th Lancers was sent to Iran to reinforce 8th Division in Persia and meet a potential German threat through the Caucasus. The following year, they returned to 8th division for operating in Italy, fighting their way north to Venice where they were stopped. 6th returned to India in June 1945.

Partition
The regiment was allotted to Pakistan.
Last dress uniform
Blue, red facings, golden lace.
Class composition (1940)
Jats, Punjabi Muslims, Sikhs.

Battle Honours
Afghanistan 1878-80, Tel-el-Kebir, E t 1882, Punjab Frontier, China 1900, Shaiba, Kut-al-Amara 1915-17, Ctesiphon, Tigris 1916, Baghdad, Sharqat, Mesopotamia 1915-18, North West Frontier, India 1915, Afghanistan 1919, The Trigno, Tufillo, The Sangro, The Moro, Cassino II, Pignataro, Liri Valley, The Senio, Santerno Crossing, Italy 1943-45.

Watson's rissaldar, 1888. (Artwork by Paul Chater)

7th Light Cavalry

Lineage

1784	2nd Regiment of Madras Native Cavalry or "Campbell Ki Pultan"
1786	1st Regiment of Madras Native Cavalry
1788	3rd Regiment of Madras Native Cavalry
1819	3rd Regiment of Madras Light Cavalry
1891	3rd Regiment of Madras Lancers
1903	28th Light Cavalry

7th Light Cavalry

One of the oldest cavalry regiments in the service of British India, it started life in the service of the Nawab of Arcot's army. In April 1784, 2nd Madras Cavalry were formed from three disbanded regiments. The corps was also called "Campbell Ki Pultan" referring to the name of its first commander.

The regiment was present during the Third Mysore War. Its first battle turned out to have a disastrous effect. The cavalry charge went too far from the lines and exposed the men to the musket fire of entrenched enemies. The regiment lost 270 horses and was dismounted. Re-equipped, it served in the Mahratta Wars and against the Pindaris. It was present at the victory of Mahidpore.

In 1915, 28th Light Cavalry – as it was renamed – established a cordon between Persia and Afghanistan. When the 1917 revolution broke out, it was confronted by the Bolshevik cavalry. The 28th is the only imperial cavalry regiment to have fought the Soviets. In 1922, the regiment became 7th Light Cavalry, one of the three regiments escaping amalgamation.

During the Second World War, the regiment was converted to an armoured unit and served in Burma with 19th and 20th Divisions. In April 1946, it formed part of the Occupation Force in Japan.

Partition
The regiment was allotted to India.
Last dress uniform
Blue, French grey facings.
Class composition (1940)
Jats, Punjabi Muslims, Sikhs.

Battle Honours
Mysore, Seringapatam, Maheidpoor, Merv, Persia 1915-19, Afghanistan 1919, Imphal, Kyaukmyaung, Mandalay, Meiktila, Rangoon Road, Burma 1942-45.

7th Light Cavalry, 1908. (Artwork by Bruno Mugnai)

8th King George V's Own Light Cavalry

Lineage

1787	5th Regiment of Madras Native Cavalry
1788	1st Regiment of Madras Native Cavalry
1819	1st Regiment of Madras Light Cavalry
1826	4th Regiment Nizam's Cavalry # IMAGE 10#
1854	4th Cavalry, Hyderabad Contingent
1886	1st Regiment Madras Lancers
1890	4th Lancers, Hyderabad Contingent
1901	26th Light Cavalry
1903	1st Madras Lancers
1903	30th Lancers (Gordon's Horse)
1906	26th Prince of Wales's Own Light Cavalry
1910	26th King George's Own Light Cavalry

The 8th KGVO Light Cavalry

The regiments which went to form 8th KGO Light Cavalry were **26th KGO Cavalry** and **30th Lancers (Gordon's Horse).**

26th Light Cavalry were raised in 1787 in Arcot as 5th Regiment of Madras Native Cavalry. Three years later, it saw its first action against Tipu, Raja of Mysore. The campaign was so hard that the regiment fought dismounted most of the time. On its way to Seringapatam, the 26th delivered a skilful charge which utterly defeated the enemy's cavalry at Malavelly. In 1826, the regiment went to Afghanistan. It fought in the second Afghan War and in Burma in 1885. A part of the regiment was sent to Aden during The First World War while a squadron went to Persia. The 26th took part in the third Afghan War of 1919.

30th Lancers saw birth in 1826 as 4th Nizam's Cavalry. From its raising until the Mutiny, the regiment was constantly in field service against the marauders of central India. The 30th was also in action against Rajah Bikbhiz Pathoor and helped to put down the rebellion of Arab mercenaries in 1841. In 1887, the regiment went to Northern Burma. As part of the Ambala Cavalry Brigade, the 30th fought in France, in the trenches of Givenchy, before sailing back to India in 1917 and getting posted to the North West Frontier.

Both corps were amalgamated in June 1921 in Peshawar.

At the outbreak of the Second World War, 8th Light Cavalry was on pacification duties in Waziristan. It was then sent to patrol the Gulf of Bengal's coastline against a potential Japanese invasion. In 1945, the 8th was detailed to join 19th Division in Burma as its reconnaissance regiment.

Partition
The regiment was allotted to India.
Last dress uniform
Blue, French grey facings.
Class composition (1940)
Jats, Punjabi Muslims, Sikhs.

Battle Honours
Mysore, Seringapatam, Ava, Central India, Afghanistan 1879-80, Burma 1885-87, Givenchy 1914, France and Flanders 1914-18, Aden, Afghanistan 1919, Sittang 1945, Burma 1942-45.

8th Light Cavalry, 1910 and 1911. (Artwork by Mike Chappell)

Royal Deccan Horse
(9th Horse)

Lineage

1826	1st Regiment of Nizam's Cavalry
1826	2nd Regiment of Nizam's Cavalry
1854	1st Cavalry, Hyderabad Contingent
1854	2nd Cavalry, Hyderabad Contingent
1890	1st Lancers, Hyderabad Contingent
1890	2nd Lancers, Hyderabad Contingent
1903	20th Deccan Horse
1903	29th Lancers (Deccan Horse)
1921	20th Royal Deccan Horse

Royal Deccan Horse

The two regiments which were amalgamated to form 9th Royal Deccan Horse were two old Hyderabad-raised regiments: **20th Royal Deccan Horse** and **29th Lancers (Deccan Horse).**

Until the end of the Mutiny, the 20th, 29th and 30th cavalry regiments shared a common background.

In 1816, the Nizam of Hyderabad had been talked into having his army commanded by the British. A selection was made in this numerous though ineffective Hyderabad's army, resulting in the creation of five cavalry regiments of the Hyderabad Contingent.

> 1st Nizam's Cavalry (1903 – 20th Deccan Horse)
> 2nd Nizam's Cavalry (1903 – 29th Deccan Horse)
> 3rd Nizam's Cavalry (1903 – disbanded)
> 4th Nizam's Cavalry (1903 – 30th Lancers)
> 5th Nizam's Cavalry (1903 – disbanded)

Until 1857, the Nizam's cavalry were permanently operating against the Pindaris who posed an ongoing threat to peace and order. During the Great Mutiny, the Contingent served in Central India.

During the First World War, the two regiments were part of the Indian Cavalry Corps and served in France before being sent to Palestine to participate in Allenby's final victorious campaign.

The amalgamation took place in July 1921 in Bolarum. 9th Deccan Horse was converted to a tank regiment in 1944 and participated as such in the Burma campaign with 255th Tank Brigade.

Partition
In 1947, the regiment was allotted to India.
Last dress uniform
Rifle green, white facings.
Class composition (1940)
Jats, Punjabi Muslims, Sikhs.

Battle Honours
Central India, Givenchy 1914, Somme 1916, Bazentin, DelvilleWood, Flers-Courcelettes, Cambrai 1917, France and Flanders 1914-18, Megiddo, Sharon, Damascus, Palestine 1918, Meiktila, Capture of Meiktila, Defence of Meiktila, Rangoon Road, Pyawbwe, Burma 1942-45.

9th Deccan Horse, 1930. (Artwork by Mike Chappell)

Guides Cavalry
(10th Queen Victoria's Own Frontier Force)

Lineage

1847	The Corps of Guides
1857	The Corps of Guides, Punjab Frontier Force
1879	The Queen's Own Corps of Guides, Punjab Frontier Force
1904	Queen's Own Corps of Guides (Lumsden's)
1911	Queen Victoria's Own corps of Guides (Frontier Force) (Lumsden's)
1921	10th Queen Victoria's Own Corps of Guides Cavalry (Frontier Force)

Guides Cavalry

On 14 December 1846, Lieutenant Lumsden was appointed commandant of a troop of Guides Cavalry (around 100 sabres strong) and of two companies of Guides Infantry, each of 100 men. Lumsden recruited his men from all the warlike hill tribes. The Guides were immediately engaged in operations against the tribesmen of the North West Frontier. The corps cavalry were present at Multan and Gujerat during the second Sikh War. On 19 June 1849, the number of men in the cavalry were increased to a total of 400 sabres.

News of the Mutiny at Meerut was confirmed at Peshawar on 12 May 1857. That evening, the Guides' 153 cavalry and 379 infantry personnel set out for Delhi and arrived on the morning of 9 June after marching 580 miles in 22 days. It was before Delhi that Juma, a water-carrier, received an award for bravery. He was made a sepoy, rose to the rank of officer and served as the model for Kipling's portrait of Gunga Din. On 14 September, the siege of Delhi came to an end and the Guides marched back to the Frontier.

By April 1858, they were in action against the rebel remnants of 55th Bengal Native Infantry. Campaigns on the Frontier followed and in 1878, war was declared against Afghanistan. After the treaty of Gandamak, the British resident marched towards Kabul with an escort of 25 sowars and 52 sepoys from the Guides. They were attacked inside the embassy by a large force of Afghan soldiers; only nine cavalrymen of the escort survived.

In 1917, the cavalry sailed to Mesopotamia. They fought the Turks in the battle of Khan Baghdadi and, in 1918, they were at Shergat, the last battle to be fought in that theatre. Later, they served in North Persia before coming back to India in 1921. The regiment then became non-*silladar* and the cavalry and infantry were separated.

During the Second World War, the Guides went briefly to Mesopotamia before serving on 8th Army's desert flank during the withdrawal to El Alamein. Shortly afterwards, they returned to India and saw no more action until the end of the war.

Partition
The regiment was allotted to Pakistan in 1947.
Last dress uniform
Drab (khaki), red facings.
Class composition (1940)
Dogras, Pathans, Sikhs.

Battle Honours
Mooltan, Goojerat, Punjaub, Delhi 1857, Ali Masjid, Kabul 1879, Afghanistan 1878-80, Chitral, Malakand, Punjab Frontier, Khan Baghdadi, Sharquat, Mesopotamia 1917-18, North West Frontier, India 1915, Bir Hacheim, Minquar Qaim, Deir el Shein, North Africa 1940-43.

10th Guides Cavalry, 1890. (Artwork by Mike Chappell)

Prince Albert Victor's Own Cavalry
(11th Frontier Force)

Lineage

1849	1st Regiment of Punjab Cavalry
1849	3rd Regiment of Punjab Cavalry
1851	1st Regiment of Cavalry, Punjab Irregular Force
1851	3rd Regiment of Cavalry, Punjab Irregular Force
1865	1st Regiment of Cavalry, Punjab Frontier Force
1865	3rd Regiment of Cavalry, Punjab Frontier Force # IMAGE 13#
1890	1st (Prince Albert Victor's Own) Regiment of Punjab Cavalry
1901	1st (Prince Albert Victor's Own) Punjab Cavalry
1901	3rd Regiment of Punjab Cavalry
1903	21st Prince Albert Victor's Own Cavalry, Frontier Force
1903	23rd Cavalry (Frontier Force)
1904	Prince Albert Victor's Own Cavalry (Frontier Force) (Daly's Horse)

Prince Albert Victor's Own Cavalry

After the annexation of the Punjab in 1849, five regiments of Irregular Cavalry were raised to protect the new frontier from the Black Mountain to the limits of Scinde. PAVO Cavalry is the descendant of the first and third of those regiments.

1st Punjab Cavalry sent down to Delhi a squadron during the Mutiny which also participated in the pacification of Oudh. The regiment fought gallantly during the second Afghan War at Ahmed Khel in April 1880. The third was engaged in the suppression of the Mutiny of 66th Bengal Native Infantry in Amritsar. It was then engaged in many minor fights on the border and served during the second Afghan War.

Both regiments were in the Mahsud campaign of 1894-1895 and in the border insurrections of 1897-1898. In 1903, 1st and 3rd Punjab Cavalry became 21st and 23rd, respectively. During the First World War, both regiments took part in the Mesopotamia campaigns and, in 1919, they were engaged in the third Afghan War. In June 1921, they were amalgamated to form 11th PAVO.

In July 1940, the regiment was mechanised and became part of 3rd Motor Brigade at Sialkot. Its first participation overseas took place in the Middle East. In 1943, the 11th returned to India and was back in action against the Japanese as the reconnaissance regiment of XXIII Corps during its trips to Imphal and Rangoon. Back to India to be re-equipped, 11th PAVO was dispatched to Singapore and later to the Dutch Indies.

Partition
The 11th PAVO was allotted to Pakistan.
Last dress uniform
Blue, scarlet facings.
Class composition (1940)
Ranghars, Hindustanis and Punjabi Muslims, Sikhs.

Battle Honours
Delhi 1857, Lucknow, Ahmad Khel, Kandahar 1880. Afghanistan 1878-80, Kut-al-Amara 1917, Baghdad, Khan Baghdadi, Sharqat, Mesopotamia 1915-18, Afghanistan 1919, El Mechili, Halfaya 1941, Bir Hacheim, North Africa 1940-43, Relief of Kohima, Monywa 1945, Mandalay, Myinmu Bridgehead, Capture of Meiktila, The Irrawaddy, Rangoon Road, Burma 1942-45

Sam Browne's Cavalry
(12th Frontier Force)

Lineage

1849	2nd Regiment of Punjab Cavalry
1849	5th Regiment of Punjab Cavalry
1851	2nd Regiment of Cavalry (Punjab Irregular Force)
1851	5th Regiment of Cavalry (Punjab Irregular Force)
1865	2nd Regiment of Cavalry, Punjab Frontier Force
1865	5th Regiment of Cavalry, Punjab Frontier Force # IMAGE 14#
1901	2nd Punjab Cavalry
1901	5th Punjab Cavalry
1903	22nd Cavalry (Frontier Force)
1903	25th Cavalry (Frontier Force)
1904	22nd Sam Browne's Cavalry (Frontier Force)

Sam Browne's Cavalry

12th Cavalry were born when **22nd Sam Browne's Cavalry** and **25th Cavalry** merged in 1921.

The **22nd** was recruited in Lahore in 1849 by Lieutenant Samuel J. Browne of 36th Bengal Native Infantry. It was initially known as 2nd Punjab Cavalry. The regiment saw service on the North West Frontier till 1857 when its squadrons participated in the reconquest of Delhi, Agra, Cawnpore and Lucknow.

In 1858, Major S. Browne lost his arm at the battle of Sarpoorah. Shortly afterwards, he invented the famous belt whose design was intended to facilitate carrying a sword and pistol. Another uniform innovation which seems to be due to the 22nd is the common use of shoulder-chains in the cavalry.

After the Mutiny, the regiment saw intensive action on the Frontier. During the second Afghan War, it distinguished itself at Ahmed Khel. In 1916, the 22nd sailed to Mesopotamia where it stayed until 1920.

25th Punjab Cavalry were raised in Multan the same year as the 22nd. Squadrons of the regiment were part of the relief column heading to Delhi. After the Mutiny, the 25th went back to the Frontier and participated in the second Afghan War where it escorted the Commander-in-Chief into Kabul. The regiment remained on the North West Frontier until 1915 after which it sailed to East Africa and was back on the Frontier just in time to resist the Afghan invasion in 1919.

In 1937, the active life of Sam Browne's Cavalry ended and the 12th became the training regiment of 2nd Indian Cavalry Group with a permanent station in Ferozepore.

Partition
The regiment was disbanded in 1947.
Last dress uniform
Scarlet, blue facings.
Class composition (1940)
??

Battle Honours
Delhi 1857, Lucknow, Charasiah, Kabul 1879, Ahmad Khal, Afghanistan 1878-80, Kut-al-Amara 1917, Baghdad, Mesopotamia 1916-18, North West Frontier, India 1914-15, East Africa 1917, Afghanistan 1919.

12th Cavalry, 1897. (Artwork by Bruno Mugnai)

13th Duke of Connaught's Own Lancers

Lineage

1817	1st Regiment of Bombay Light Cavalry
1817	2nd Regiment of Bombay Light Cavalry
1842	1st Regiment of Bombay Light Cavalry (Lancers)
1861	1st Regiment of Bombay Silladar Light Cavalry
1862	1st Regiment of Bombay Light Cavalry
1880	1st Bombay Lancers
1880	2nd Bombay Lancers
1890	1st (Duke of Connaught's Own) Bombay Lancers
1903	31st Duke of Connaught's Own Lancers
1903	32nd Lancers

13th Duke of Connaught's Own Lancers

The union of **31st DCO Lancers** and **32nd Lancers** was a natural one. Both regiments had had a common origin in the old Bombay Squadron of Cavalry, raised in 1803 after an unsuccessful attempt to create a European cavalry unit. A second troop was organised in 1816, and in 1817 the two troops became regiments by the addition of volunteers from 2nd and 4th Madras Cavalry and from Poona Auxiliary Force.

The first regiment went to Afghanistan in 1839 and was present at the conquest of Ghuznee. The regiment was converted to lancers in 1842. During the Mutiny, the 31st remained loyal. In 1862, it became *silladar*. Detachments fought in Burma in 1885. The First World War saw the regiment patrolling the North West Frontier and taking a brilliant part in the third Afghan War.

32nd Lancers found its origin in the second troop which became 2nd Regiment Bombay Light Cavalry in 1817. Until 1838, both regiments were in action in Gujerat, Sind and at Kathiawar. During the Mutiny, the 32nd, which remained loyal, captured the Fort of Nimbhara. It served during the second Afghan War and participated in the occupation of Kandahar. It sailed to Mesopotamia in 1917 and was one of the first units to enter Baghdad. On 22 April 1917, a mounted charge led by the colonel against an entrenched Turkish position resulted in all the officers and almost all the men becoming casualties. Before returning to India, the regiment saw heavy fighting in the Kurdish rebellion.

The amalgamation took place in September 1923. In April 1941, 13th Lancers sailed to Iraq with 10th Division. They fought in Syria against the French Vichy forces and subsequently joined 8th Army. They left Egypt before the battle of El Alamein and moved on to Java in support of 5th and 23rd Divisions.

Partition
The regiment joined the Pakistan army in 1947.
Last dress uniform
Blue, scarlet facings.
Class composition (1940)
Pathans, Ranghars, Sikhs.

Battle Honours
Ghuznee, Afghanistan 1839, Mooltan, Punjaub, Central India, Afghanistan 1878-80, Burma 1885¬87, Kut al Amara 1917, Baghdad, Sharqat, Mesopotamia 1916-18, North West Frontier, India 1917, Afghanistan 1919, North West Frontier 1937-40, Damascus, Deir es Zor, Raqaa, Syria 1941, Gazala, Bir Hacheim, El Adem, Gambut, Sidi Rezegh 1942, Tobruck 1942, Fuka, North Africa 1940-43.

13th Cavalry. (Artwork by Vallet)

Scinde Horse
(14th Prince of Wales's Own Cavalry)

Lineage

1838	Scinde Irregular Horse
1846	1st Scinde Horse
1846	2nd Scinde Horse
1885	5th Bombay Cavalry # IMAGE 16#
1885	6th Bombay Cavalry
1888	5th Scinde Horse
1888	6th Jacob's Horse
1903	35th Scinde Horse
1903	36th Jacob's Horse

Scinde Horse

The regiment was made up of 35th Scinde Horse and 36th Jacob's Horse.

A detachment of Poona Horse became the nucleus of Scinde Irregular Horse in 1838, and the regiment was so efficient in its operations to bring peace and order in the Sind that the command decided to raise a second one.

The 1st regiment served in Persia in 1857 and was brought back to fight the mutineers. The second regiment kept position on the Baluch border. In 1885, both regiments were renamed 5th and 6th Bombay Cavalry respectively and, three years later, they became 5th Scinde Horse and 6th Jacob's Horse. When the reorganisation took place in 1903, they were renumbered 35th and 36th.

During the First World War, the 35th stayed in India. It was sent to Mesopotamia in 1920 where it was constantly engaged in putting down the Arab rising and relieving besieged places. The 36th was part of Lucknow Brigade/1st Cavalry Division which fought in France until 1917 and took a remarkable part in General Allenby's victorious drive in Palestine.

The amalgamation took place in 1921 at Jubbolpore. During the Second World War, the regiment spent two years on the Frontier before going on to serve in Paiforce, Egypt and Syria.

Partition
The regiment was allotted to India.
Last dress uniform
Dark blue, red facings.
Class composition (1940)
Pathans, Ranghars, Sikhs.

Battle Honours
Meeanee, Hyderabad, Cutchee, Mooltan, Goojerat, Punjaub, Persia, Central India, Afghanistan 1878-80, Somme 1916, Morval, Cambrai 1917, France and Flanders 1914-18, Megiddo, Sharon, Damascus, Palestine 1918, North West Frontier, India 1914-15, 1918.

14th Scinde Horse, 1920 and 1939. (Artwork by Mike Chappell)

15th Lancers

Lineage

1858	Robart's Horse
1861	17th Bengal Cavalry
1885	17th Bengal Lancers
1885	7th Bombay Cavalry #IMAGE 17#
1886	7th Bombay Cavalry (Baluch Horse)
1890	7th Bombay Lancers
1903	17th Cavalry
1903	37th Lancers (Baluch Horse

15th Lancers

The regiment was born from the amalgamation of **17th Cavalry** and **37th Lancers.**

17th Cavalry were raised in 1857 from Muttra Horse and Rohilkhand Police and became Robart's Horse the following year. Colonel Robart, the first commandant, possessed large private means and was lavish with his money: he melded the corps into a crack unit of the new Bengal Army. The men received their baptism of fire during the Bhutan expedition of 1866. The regiment fought the second Afghan War but was disembodied in June 1881 for economic reasons. Fearing a war against Russia, the regiment would be restored four years later.

17th Cavalry were unlucky: it was unable to play a role in the First World War because of disease and epidemics. In the meantime, a Pathan squadron went overseas to East Africa where they fought until January 1917. In 1919, the war with Afghanistan gave the regiment plenty to do.

37th Lancers (Baluch Horse) was raised in 1885 as 7th Bombay Cavalry. They saw no service until 1919. Operations during the third Afghan War gave the regiment, as a whole, no opportunity to show their mettle.

The two corps were merged at Lucknow in February 1922 to form 15th Lancers.

In 1937, the regiment became the permanent training centre of Jhansi's First Cavalry Group.

Partition
The regiment was disbanded in 1947.
Last dress uniform
Blue, buff facings.

Battle Honours
Afghanistan 1879-80, Afghanistan 1919.

A Jemadar of 7th Bombay Lancers, Diamond Jubilee 1897. (Artwork by John Charlton)

16th Light Cavalry

Lineage

1776	3rd Nawab of Arcot Cavalry
1784	3rd Regiment of Madras Native Cavalry
1787	1st Regiment of Madras Native Cavalry
1788	2nd Regiment of Madras Native Cavalry
1860	2nd Madras Cavalry
1886	2nd Madras Lancers
1903	27th Light Cavalry

16th Light Cavalry

16th Light Cavalry was the oldest cavalry regiment in the Indian Army. It is believed to have been raised around 1776, when they were formed as the 3rd Cavalry in the service of the Nawab of Arcot. The Company decided to take them into their own service in 1780. They fought at Sholinghur and were the only cavalry regiment to bear honours for that victory.

In 1784, the regiment was re-named 3rd Madras Native Cavalry. A mutiny amongst the Madras regiments led to some disbandment, giving the 3rd the opportunity to become number two in the ranking.

The regiment took part in the war against Tipu of Mysore in 1790 and it joined the army of Deccan for service against the Mahrattas in 1799. Split up into detachments, it joined the conquest of Upper Burma in 1886.

The abolition of separate armies in 1903 changed the title to 27th Light Cavalry which was retained until 1922.

The First World War gave the 27th few opportunities: they sent their machine-gun section for service with the Hariana Lancers: one squadron proceeded to Persia and another formed part of the punitive expedition against the Marris on the North West Frontier.

In 1919, when the Afghans invaded India, the regiment was at once despatched and led two decisive charges against the tribal cavalry. Then the regiment destroyed the capital of the Sherranis during a brilliant night manœuvre (24-25 June 1919). The regiment was only mechanised in 1941. It served in Burma and led the progression to Rangoon before joining the Occupation Force from French Indochina until October 1946.

Partition
The regiment was allotted to India.
Last dress uniform
Blue, French grey facings.
Class composition (1940)
Jats, Rajput, Rajputana Muslims.

Battle Honours
Sholinghur, Carnatic, Mysore, Seringapatam, Burma 1885-87, Afghanistan 1919, Meiktila, Capture of Meiktila, Defence of Meiktila, Pegu 1945, Sittang 1945, Rangoon Road, Burma 1942-45.

16th Light Cavalry. (Artwork by Mike Chappell)

Poona Horse
(17th Queen Victoria's Own Cavalry)

Lineage

1817	Poona Auxiliary Horse
1820	3rd Bombay Light Cavalry
1839	4th Bombay Cavalry (Poona Horse)
1876	3rd (Queen's Own) Bombay Light Cavalry
1892	4th (Prince Albert Victor's Own) Bombay Cavalry (Poona Horse)
1903	33rd Queen's Own Light Cavalry
1903	34th Prince Albert Victor's Own Poona Horse
1914	33rd Queen Victoria's Own Light Cavalry

Poona Horse (17th Queen Victoria's Own Cavalry)

Poona Horse had more battle honours than any other cavalry regiment in the Queen's service. The regiment was born from the merger of **33rd QVO Cavalry** with **34th PAVO Poona Horse.**

33rd Queen Victoria's Own Light Cavalry was raised in 1820 as 3rd Bombay Light Cavalry. It took part in the battles of Ghuznee and Kabul in 1842. During the Scinde war of 1842, 3rd Bombay was part of the charge leading to the victory of Hyderabad.

When the Shah of Persia invaded Herat in 1856, the regiment participated in the battles of Reshire, Bushire and finally in the victory of Kushab. In 1858, 3rd Bombay operated against the fleeing mutineers in Central India. Ten years later, they were in Abyssinia to punish King Theodore. The regiment saw action during the second Afghan War and was part of the expedition against the Boxers in China. In 1914, the 33rd was the first to land in Mesopotamia. Back in India, they led the Indian Army's offensive during the third Afghan War and were with the strike force invading Dhaka.

34th Prince Albert Victor's Own Poona Horse found its origins in the *risallahs* formed in the territory of the Peshwa of Poona in 1817. These units distinguished themselves in the battle of Corygaum. From 1820 until the First World War, both regiments shared the same campaigns with only two exceptions: Abyssinia and China. In 1914, the 34th sailed to France to participate in the battles of La Bassée and Armentières. They fought on the Somme and finally joined the Desert Mounted Corps as part of 14th Cavalry Brigade.

In 1921, the two regiments were amalgamated to form 17th QVO Cavalry. April 1942 saw Poona Horse in Bassorah with 252nd Armoured Brigade before moving to Egypt to become the reconnaissance regiment of XXXth corps. In September 1942, they were posted to Iran with 6th Division and finally ended the war in Cyprus.

Partition

The Poona Horse was allotted to the Indian Army.

Last dress uniform

Dark blue, French grey facings.

Class composition (1940)

Jats, Rajput, Kaimkhani.[3]

Battle Honours

Corygaum, Ghuznee 1839, Afghanistan 1839, Kandahar 1842, Ghuznee 1842, Cabool 1842, Meeanee, Hyderabad, Reshire, Bushire, Kooshab, Persia, Central India, Abyssinia, Kandahar 1880, Afghanistan 1878-80, China 1900, La Bassee 1914, Armentieres 1914, Somme 1916, Bazentin, Flers-Courcelettes, Cambrai 1917, France and Flanders 1914-18, Megiddo, Sharon, Damascus, Palestine 1918, Shaiba, Ctesiphon, Tigris 1916, Mesopotamia 1914-16, Afghanistan 1919, North Africa 1940-43.

---

3   Muslim clan of Rajputana.

17th Poona Horse, 1890 and 1915. (Artwork by Mike Chappell)

18th King Edward VII's Own Cavalry

Lineage

1842	8th Bengal Irregular Cavalry
1846	16th Bengal Irregular Cavalry
1846	17th Bengal Irregular Cavalry
1861	6th Bengal Cavalry
1861	7th Bengal Cavalry
1882	6th Prince of Wales's Own Bengal Cavalry
1903	6th Prince of Wales's Own Cavalry
1903	7th Hariana Lancers
1906	6th King Edward's Own Cavalry

The 18th King Edward VII's Own Cavalry

The two regiments which became 18th Cavalry were **6th KEO Cavalry** and **7th Hariana Lancers.**

6th King Edward's Own Cavalry   As a result of the set-backs suffered in Afghanistan and the seriousness of the internal situation in India, new regiments were raised. 8th Bengal Irregular Cavalry was formed in 1842. They were first blooded at Punniar during the war against Gwalior. After this war, came the first Sikh war.

When the Mutiny broke out, most of the Indian officers stood firm even if the greater part of the troopers had deserted. The threat of disbandment was there but the subsequent behaviour of the regiment in the Oudh campaign dismissed any idea of sanctions.

In 1861, the 8th was renumbered 6th. They saw no action until 1882 when they fought at Tel-el-Kebir and garrisoned in Cairo. In 1897, they were in several actions in the Kurram Valley. During the Great War, 6th KEO fought in France and Palestine with 2nd Cavalry Brigade. After the war, they remained in the Middle East and in Egypt until 1920.

7th Hariana Lancers   The need of more troops to control the newly occupied Punjab led to the raising of 16th Irregular Cavalry in 1846. Renumbered 17th, the regiment was on the North West Frontier in 1857 and was not tempted by the Mutiny.

In 1861, the 17th was renamed 7th Bengal Cavalry. They participated in the Burma campaign (1886-1887). In 1914, they were despatched to Mesopotamia and were reinforced by the machine-gun detachment of 27th Light Cavalry. The 7th took part in the battle of Shaiba. They were the only cavalry unit present at the first capture of Kut-el-Amara and proceeded on to Ctesiphon. A squadron was captured by the Turks in April 1916 in Kut. The other squadrons returned to India in October 1916.

In 1921, the two regiments amalgamated in Risalpur.

In January 1941, 18th Cavalry landed in Egypt. They were besieged in Tobruk for five months until relieved in August 1941. Attacked by the Axis force, the regiment responded by destroying sixty enemy tanks. Back in India in August 1942, 18th Cavalry saw no more action until the end of the war.

Partition
The regiment was allotted to India.
Last dress uniform
Dark blue, French grey facings, golden laces.
Class composition (1940)
Jats, Rajput, Kaimkhani.

Battle Honours
Punniar, Moodkee, Ferozeshah, Sobraon, Punjaub, Tel-el-Kebir, Egypt 1882, Burma 1885-87, Punjab Frontier, Somme 1916, Morval, Cambrai 1917, France and Flanders 1914-18, Megiddo, Sharon, Damascus, Palestine 1918, Shaiba, Kut-al-Amara 1915, Ctesiphon, Tigris 1916, Mesopotamia 1915-16, El Mechili, The Kennels, Defence of Tobruk, North Africa 1940-43.

19th King George V's Own Lancers

Lineage

1858	Tiwana Horse
1858	2nd Mahratta Horse
1860	Fane's Horse
1861	18th Bengal Cavalry
1861	19th Bengal Cavalry (Lancers)
1880	18th Bengal Lancers
1880	19th Bengal Lancers (Fane's Horse)
1903	18th Tiwana Lancers
1903	19th Lancers (Fane's Horse)
1906	18th (Prince of Wales's Own) Tiwana Lancers
1914	18th King George's Own Lancers

19th King George V's Own Lancers

The two regiments which went to form the 19th Lancers were **18th KGO Lancers** and **19th Fane's Horse.**

18th King George's Own Lancers was originally raised as the 2nd Mahratta Horse in 1858 for duty in central India. A detachment of Tiwana Horse was subsequently attached and the unit became 18th Bengal Cavalry after the Mutiny. During the Afghan War, the 18th was employed in keeping communications open. They did all the hard work as divisional cavalry to the Tirah expedition during the general Frontier blaze of 1897-1898. When the Great War started, the regiment sailed to France and was in the Meerut Brigade of 2nd Cavalry Division. They participated in all the actions of the Cavalry Corps in France and Palestine before returning to India in November 1920.

19th Lancers (Fane's Horse) was raised by Lieutenant Fane for service in China in 1859. Its ranks were mainly filled from 3rd Regiment of Hodson's Horse. The regiment played an important part in the seizure of the Taku forts and in the march to Peking. On its return to India, the regiment was renamed 19th Bengal Cavalry. It participated with distinction in the second Afghan War and won decorations in Ahmed Kehl. In 1914, the regiment was posted to the Sialkot Brigade of 1st Cavalry Division. Along with the 18th, they were involved in all fights of the Cavalry Corps and returned to India in 1921.

The two regiments were amalgamated in August 1921 in New Delhi.

At the end of 1941, the regiment joined 1st Armoured Division as its reconnaissance regiment (the division was renumbered 31st Division in 1942). 19th Lancers moved to Madras on coast-watch duties before joining 50th Indian Tank Brigade. It then fought in the Arakan taking part in the capture of Akyab, and landed in Ramree and Rangoon with the 26th Division.

Partition
The regiment went to Pakistan in 1947.
Last dress uniform
Scarlet, white facings, gold lace.
Class composition (1940)
Jats, Sikhs, Punjabi Muslims.

Battle Honours
Taku Forts, Pekin 1860, Ahmad Khel, Afghanistan 1878-80, Tirah, Punjab Frontier, Somme 1916, Bazentin, Flers-Courcelettes, Morval, Cambrai 1917, France & Flanders 1914-18, Megiddo, Sharon, Damascus, Palestine 1918, Buthidaung, Rangoon Road, Mayu Valley, Myebon, Kangaw, Ru-Ywa, Dalet, Tarnandu, Burma 1942-45.

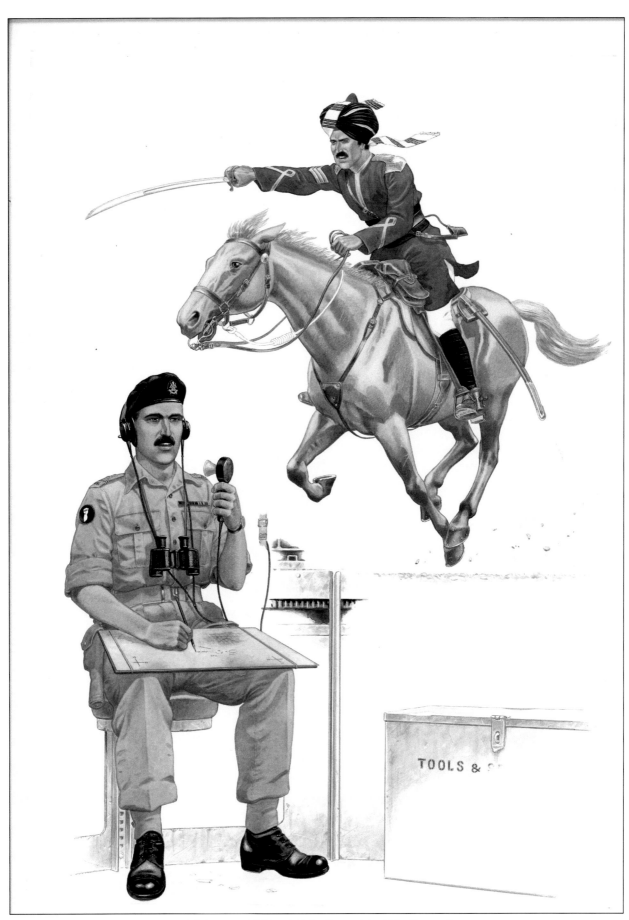

19th Lancers, 1905 and 1945. (Artwork by Mike Chappell)

20th Lancers

Lineage

1857	Jat Horse Yeomanry
1857	Multani Regiment of Cavalry
1861	14th Bengal Lancers (Murray's Jat Horse)
1861	15th Bengal Lancers (Cureton's Multanis)
1903	14th Murray's Jat Lancers
1903	15th Lancers (Cureton's Multanis)

20th Lancers

Both regiments which formed 20th Lancers were born during the Great Mutiny. Moreover, both of them were single class regiments: **14th Murray's Jat Lancers** consisted of Hindu Jats only while **15th Lancers (Cureton's Multanis)** comprised Multani Pathans and related tribes.

14th Murray's Jat was born from the Jat Horse Yeomanry raised in 1857. They served in Bhutan and in the second Afghan War. During the Great War, they were at the North West Frontier fighting the Mohmands in 1915. In 1916, they were detailed to Mesopotamia as part of 7th Cavalry Brigade and took part in the operation leading to the capture of Baghdad and cutting off the Turkish retreat.

15th Lancers was formed from *rissalahs* of Baluch and Pathan tribesmen to fight the mutineers in 1857. Like the 14th, they served in Central India and in the second Afghan War. The Cureton's Multanis were the first cavalrymen to land in France in 1914 where they became the divisional cavalry of the Lahore Division. Leaving France in December 1915, they proceeded to Persia, where they remained as part of the blockading cordon to keep enemy propagandists out of Afghanistan.

Both regiments were amalgamated in 1920 in Sialkot. In 1937, they became the training regiment for 3rd Indian Cavalry Group at Lucknow.

Partition
The regiment was disbanded in 1947.
Last dress uniform
Blue, scarlet facings.

Battle Honours
Charasiah, Kabul 1879, Afghanistan 1878-80, Neuve Chapelle, France & Flanders 1914-15, Kut-al-Amara 1917, Sharqat, Mesopotamia 1916-18, Persia 1916-19, North-West Frontier, India 1915.

Central India Horse
(21st King George V's Own Horse)

Lineage

1858	Mayne's Horse
1861	1st Central India Horse
1861	2nd Central India Horse
1903	38th Central India Horse
1903	39th Central India Horse
1906	38th Prince of Wales's Own Central India Horse
1906	39th Prince of Wales's Own Central India Horse

Central India Horse (21st King George V's Own Horse)

38th and **39th Central India Horse** were amalgamated to form 21st Regiment.

Composed of loyal elements from various cavalry units, the Central India Horse was raised in 1858. Both regiments were in action during the second Afghan War and were later formed as a composite unit which was deployed on the North West Frontier.

In 1911, the 39th was despatched for two years to Persia for the purpose of protecting threatened British citizens. The 39th remained in India for the duration of the war, training officers, men and horses.

In October 1914, the 38th was mobilised as part of the Mhow Brigade of 2nd Cavalry Division for service in France. They were decimated at Cambrai but, re-equipped, they were in the van of the cavalry in the Palestine offensive. The regiment served in Syria until 1921.

The amalgamation into one regiment took place at Quetta in 1921. The Central India Horse was the first cavalry regiment to sail overseas in July 1940. It fought with 5th Division in Abyssinia, at the relief of Tobruk, in North Africa, in Italy and ended the war in Greece.

Partition
The regiment was allotted to India.
Last dress uniform
Khaki, maroon facings, gold lace.
Class composition (1940)
Dogras,[4] Jats, Punjabi Muslims.

Battle Honours
Kandahar 1880, Afghanistan 1879-80, Punjab Frontier, Somme 1916, Morval Cambrai 1917, France and Flanders 1914-18, Megiddo, Sharon, Damascus, Palestine 1918, Keren-Asmara Road, Abyssinia 1940-41, Relief of Tobruk 1941, North Africa 1940-43, Gothic Line, Italy 1944-45, Greece 1944-45.

---

4   The Dogra squadron of the 11th PAVO replaced the Sikh squadron which had refused to embark at Bombay.

21st Central India Horse, 1897, 1912 and 1945. (Artwork by Mike Chappell)

4

The Infantry

It is important to note that the main reorganisations of the Indian Army resulted in units being renamed and renumbered.

1796

In all three armies, battalions were grouped in pairs to form regiments with one list of officers. There was a colonel for the regiment and 44 British officers, 22 to each battalion. For example: 4th Battalion, raised in 1758 in Bengal, became 1st Battalion, 2nd Regiment, Bengal Native Infantry; in the Madras Army, 3rd Battalion Coast Sepoys, raised in 1759, became 1st Battalion, 2nd Madras Native Infantry.

1824

In all three armies, the battalions became separate again, each with 22 officers in a separate list.

In Bengal: the 1st/2nd became the 5th Regiment Bengal Native Infantry, the 2nd/15th became the 31st.

In Madras: the 1st/2nd became 2nd Madras Native Infantry.

1860-1863

Several changes occurred after the Mutiny. The Bengal line now began as follows:

The former 21st became the 1st
The former 31st became the 2nd
The former 43rd became 6th Bengal Light Infantry
and so on and so forth
The regiments which had not mutinied remained unchanged

14th Bengal Native Infantry in 1861 were Ferozepore Sikhs (Brasyer's Sikhs) and. from then on, the numbers refer to regiments raised after the Sikh Wars or in the Punjab during the Mutiny. Until 1903, the list is chaotic; the Punjab Irregular Frontier Force is numbered separately, as are the Gurkhas (though 3rd Gurkhas were once 18th Bengal NI and 9th Gurkhas were 9th Bengal Native Infantry) and the Hyderabad Contingent. Bombay regiments, on the whole, kept their numbers between 1824 and 1903.

1903

All battalions (except the Gurkhas) were renumbered consecutively from the 1st Brahmans to the 130th Baluchis. The following numbering method was applied:

Bengal army – nos. 1 to 50,
Punjab Frontier Force – nos. 51 to 59,
Madras army – nos. 61 to 88,
Burman regiment – no. 93,
Hyderabad Contingent – nos. 94 to 99,
Bombay army – nos. 101 to 130.
Gurkhas remained numbered from 1 to 10.

Until 1914

Most of the infantry regiments had only one battalion, only the Gurkhas and the Garhwal Rifles had two. The regular strength of the infantry battalion was:

13 British officers,

17 Indian officers,

723 NCOs and privates, all Indians.

During the War

Indian battalions were brought into line with the British practice of four companies per battalion. Each company consisted of four platoons and each platoon consisted of four sections. All battalion and company commanders were British. The platoons were commanded by Indian officers.

Twenty-three new regiments were raised while the regular regiments set up many new battalions. Most of these wartime-raised units were disbanded between 1919 and 1921.

Wartime-raised regiments

1916   The Machine-Gun Corps

1917   49th Bengalis

        50th Kumaon

        70th Burma Rifles

        71st Coorg Rifles (Punjab Christian Battalion)

        85th Burman Rifles

        111th Mahar

1918   131st ex-Police United Provinces

        132nd ex-Police Punjab

        133rd Infantry

        140th Patiala (IST)

        141st Bikaner (IST)

        142nd Jodhpur (IST)

        143rd Narshingh (Dohlpur) (IST)

        144th Bharatpur (IST)

        145th Alwar (Jai Paltan) (IST)

        150th Infantry

        151st Infantry

        152nd Infantry

        153rd Infantry

        154th Infantry

        155th Infantry

        156th Infantry

        11th Gurkha Rifles

Regiments disbanded

3rd Brahmans,

5th Light Infantry,

17th Infantry (The Loyal Regiment),

42nd Deoli Regiment,

43rd Erinpura Regiment,

44th Merwara Infantry,

63rd Palamcottah LI,

80th Carnatic Infantry

88th Carnatic Infantry

1922

During the last major reorganisation before Independence, battalions were grouped into regiments (usually five or six active battalions and a training battalion). The 130 infantry battalions were grouped into 20 large new regiments with one battalion (the 10th) serving as permanent regimental depot and training centre.

During the Second World War, the term "10th Battalion" was set aside in favour of "Regimental Centre". The reorganisation also led to the formation of a Territorial Force similar to the British Territorial Force (it was numbered beginning with the 11th Battalion of each regiment). The new organisation decided on the disbandment of a few units and the amalgamation of almost all remaining battalions.

Pioneer Regiments in 1922:

1st Madras Pioneers
1/1st Madras from 61st Pioneers (KGO)
2/1st Madras from 64th Pioneers
10/1st Madras from 81st Pioneers
2nd Bombay Pioneers
1/2nd Bombay from 107th Pioneers
2/2nd Bombay from 12th Pioneers
3/2nd Bombay from 128th Pioneers
4/2nd Bombay from 48th Pioneers
10/2nd Bombay from 121st Pioneers
3rd Sikh Pioneers
1/3rd Sikh from 23rd Sikh Pioneers
2/3rd Sikh from 32nd Sikh Pioneers
3/3rd Sikh from 34th Sikh Pioneers
10/3rd Sikh from 2/23rd Sikh Pioneers
4th Hazara Pioneers
1/4th Hazara from 106th Hazara Pioneers

Pioneer battalions became gradually less trained in an infantry role. They were more and more used as sappers and therefore, they were grouped into four Pioneer regiments and were later absorbed by the Engineer Corps.

Organisation Infantry Regiments 1922:

The 1st Punjab Regiment
The 2nd Punjab Regiment
The 3rd Madras Regiment (disbanded in 1928)
The 4th Bombay Grenadiers
The 5th Mahratta Light Infantry
The 6th Rajputana Rifles
The 7th Rajput Regiment
The 8th Punjab Regiment
The 9th Jat Regiment
The 10th Baluch Regiment
The 11th Sikh Regiment
The12th Frontier Force Regiment
The 13th Frontier Force Rifles
The 14th Punjab Regiment
The 15th Punjab Regiment
The 16th Punjab Regiment
The 17th Dogra Regiment
The 18th Royal Garhwal Rifles
The 19th Hyderabad Regiment (later the Kumaon Regiment)
The 20th Burma Rifles

During the Second World War, recruitment was expanded to include classes which were not considered as martial races. New units bearing exotic names were raised: Ajmer, Assam, Bihar, Chamar and Mahal regiments – Coorg and Lingayat battalions.

In 1941, the Indian Army went so far as to train a parachute brigade of three battalions.

1946

In 1946, all infantry regiments, except Punjab units, lost their serial numbers retaining only their regional titles.

The 1st Punjab Regiment

The 2nd Punjab Regiment

The Madras Regiment (re-raised 1941)

The Bombay Grenadiers

The Mahratta Light Infantry

The Rajputana Rifles

The Rajput Regiment

The 8th Punjab Regiment

The Jat Regiment

The Baluch Regiment

The Sikh Regiment

The Frontier Force Regiment

The Frontier Force Rifles

The 14th Punjab Regiment

The 15th Punjab Regiment

The 16th Punjab Regiment

The Dogra Regiment

The Royal Garhwal Rifles

The Kumaon Regiment

1st Punjab Regiment

BATTALIONS	PREVIOUS TITLE (1903)	19TH CENTURY TITLE
1st Battalion	62nd Punjabis	2nd Madras Infantry
2nd Battalion	66th Punjabis	6th Madras Infantry
3rd Battalion	76th Punjabis	16th Madras Infantry
4th Battalion*	1st Brahmans	1st Brahman Infantry
5th Battalion	82nd Punjabis	22nd Madras Infantry
10th Training Battalion	84th Punjabis	24th Madras Infantry
* disbanded in 1932		

The traditions of the regiment were founded by the soldiers of Madras. 1st Battalion fought from 1767 until 1769 in the war against Hyder Ali. 1st and 2nd Battalions were present at the siege of Pondicherry in 1778. They participated with 3rd Battalion in the conquest of the city in 1780 and in operations which resulted in the victory of Sholinghur.

From 1790 until 1792, the first four battalions played an important part in the war of Mysore. They participated in the seizure of Seringapatam which ended the war in 1799.

In 1803, 1st and 10th Battalions were integrated into Wellesley's army which assaulted the fort of Ahmednagar. During that campaign, the regiment won the Assaye honour and adopted the elephant badge. The Leswaree and Bhurtpore honours were won by 4th Battalion.

The first Burma expedition saw the presence of 3rd, 5th and 10th Battalions. 1st and 2nd Battalions were part of the army which seized Nankin in 1840. The 1857 Mutiny affected the regiments of the Madras army. 2nd and 3rd Battalions went to Burma in 1885.

In 1903, the Madras regiments were converted to Punjabis and saw no more action until 1914.

First World War

1st and 3rd Battalions served in Egypt, in the Suez Canal zone and in Mesopotamia. 2nd and 3rd Battalions were, unfortunately, captured at Kut-el-Amara in November 1915 and suffered the hardships of captivity. Both battalions were reconstituted in India.

When the Afghans attempted their invasion of India in 1919, companies of 3rd Battalion were shut up in Jandola and relieved by 2nd Battalion. 11th Territorial Battalion was raised in 1921. In 1937, all company officers of 2nd Battalion were Indians.

Second World War

1st Battalion – Egypt, Iraq, Burma, Singapore, Indonesia.

2nd Battalion – Burma. It was the most decorated unit of the Indian Army.

3rd Battalion – Egypt and Italy. It was converted to an airborne role in 1946.

5th Battalion – Burma. It was part of the occupation force in Japan.

Wartime-raised units: 6th, 7th, 8th, 9th, 11th, 14th, 15th, 16th, 25th and 26th Battalions were raised for the war and disbanded when the war ended. 7th Battalion became regular in 1945.

Partition
The 1st Punjab Regiment went to the Pakistan army (1st, 2nd, 3rd, 5th and 7th Battalions).
Last dress uniform
Scarlet, green facings.
Class composition (1940)
Punjabi Muslims, Hazaras, Rajput and Sikhs.

Battle Honours
Sholinghur, Carnatic, Seringapatam, Mysore, Assaye, Laswarrie, Bourbon, Nagpore, Arakan, Ava, Bhurtpore, China, Burma 1885-87.
Suez Canal, Egypt 1915, Aden, Shaiba, Kut-al-Amara 1915-17, Defence of Kut-al-Amara, Ctesiphon, Tigris 1916, Baghdad, Mesopotamia 1915-18, NW Frontier India 1915, Afghanistan 1919.
Agordat, Keren, Kissoue, Damascus, Sidi Barrani, Tobruk 1941, Omars, Alem Harnza, Gazala, Carmusa, Defence of Alamein Line, Ruweisat Ridge, El Alamein, Montone, Gothic Line, Lamone Crossing, Pideura, Singapore Island, Pyuntaza-Shwegyin, Yenangyaung 1942, Monywa 1942, Donbaik, Htizwe, North Arakan, Razabil, Mayu Tunnels, Ngakyedauk Pass, Imphal, Litan, Kohima, Defence of Kohima, Kennedy Peak, Meiktila, Taungtha, Rangoon Road, Shwemyo Bluff, Sittang 1945, Arakan Beaches, Ramree, Burma 1942-45.

1st Punjabis, 1930 and 1919. (Artwork by Bruno Mugnai)

2nd Punjab Regiment

BATTALIONS	PREVIOUS TITLE (1903)	19TH CENTURY TITLE
1st Battalion	67th Punjabis (1st battalion in 1914-1918)	7th Madras Infantry
2nd Battalion		9th Madras Infantry
3rd Battalion	69th Punjabis	12th Burma Infantry (1885)
4th Battalion (*)	72nd Punjabis	14th Madras Infantry
5th Battalion (**)	74th Punjabis	24th Madras Infantry
10th Training Battalion	87th Punjabis	7th Madras Infantry
	67th Punjabis (2nd battalion in 1914-1918)	
(*) disbanded in 1939		
(**) disbanded in 1945		

2nd Punjab Regiment was also of old Madras origin. The first four battalions were raised between 1751 and 1776. All of them fought the wars against Mysore and the Mahrattas. The 2nd and the 3rd were captured by Hyder Ali and the French. Raised again in 1773, they found and took back their lost colours when Pondicherry was captured. In 1796, 2nd Battalion took part in the Ceylon and Amboyna expedition against the Dutch.

5th Battalion was born in 1798 and, along with the 4th, took part in the second Mahratta War, seizing the Maheidpoor batteries in 1817.

In 1824, 2nd and 3rd Battalions sailed to Burma giving the 3rd the opportunity to adopt the badge of a galley. 4th Battalion went to China to participate in the Opium War. In 1852, 2nd Battalion went back to Burma and suffered heavy losses in small scale operations.

The Madras units remained loyal during the rebellion. 5th Battalion was the only Madras unit in Lucknow operations. The hostile attitude of Burma towards India called, once again, for the services of 3rd and 4th Battalions. The state of Burma required the presence of a permanent local force and, as a result, 3rd Battalion was allocated as the 12th Burma Infantry.

First World War

The regiment's battalions were active in all theatres of operations:

the 2nd was first to sail overseas, taking part in operations in Aden, the Suez Canal zone, the Dardanelles, France and finally Mesopotamia – back in India, it participated in the third Afghan War;

the 1st went to Iraq only to be captured in Kut;

the 3rd participated in the victorious campaign in Palestine;

the 4th was garrisoned in Hong Kong and joined the 3rd in Palestine;

the 5th kept an eye on the tribes of the North West Frontier until being required in Mesopotamia in 1917. They did a great job in the Kurdish revolt and saw much fighting in the Arab rebellion of 1920-1921.

During the interwar period, all battalions took an active part in small wars on the North West Frontier.

Second World War

1st Battalion went to Aden, Somalia, Italian East Africa, Egypt and Italy. 2nd Battalion was present in Ceylon and Burma. 3rd Battalion fought in Eritrea and Egypt. Returning to India, it went on to serve in Burma and Indonesia. 5th Battalion was captured in Singapore by the Japanese.

Wartime-raised units: six additional battalions were raised: the 6th, 7th, 8th, 25th, 26th and 27th. The 27th became the Chamar Regiment in 1943 and served in Burma.

Partition
2nd Punjab Regiment was allotted to India (1st, 2nd, 3rd and 7th Battalions).
Last dress uniform
Scarlet, green facings.
Class composition (1940)
Dogras, Punjabi Muslims and Sikhs.

Battle Honours
Sholinghur, Carnatic, Mysore, Maheidpoor, Ava, China, Pegu, Lucknow, Burma 1885-87.
Loos, France and Flanders 1915, Helles, Krithia, Gallipoli 1915, Suez Canal, Egypt 1915, Megiddo Sharon, Nablus, Palestine 1918, Aden, Defence of Kut-al-Amara, Kut-al-Amara 1917, Baghdad, Mesopotamia 1915-18, NW Frontier India 1915, 1916-17, Afghanistan 1919.
Gogni, Agordat, Keren, Ad Teclesan, Berbera, Amba Alagi, Abyssinia 1940-41, British Somaliland 1940, North Africa 1940-43, Pratelle Pass, San Martino-Sogliano, Casa Bettini, Idice Bridgehead, Italy 1943-45, Central Malaya, Ipoh, Singapore Island, Malaya 1941-42, Buthidaung, Point 551, Ngakyedauk Pass, Imphal, Litan, Kanglatongbi, Tengnoupal, Kennedy Peak, Tongzang, Kangaw, Defence of Meiktila, Pyinmana, Burma 1942-45

2nd Punjabis, 1905, 1912 and 1941. (Artwork by Mike Chappell)

3rd Madras Regiment

BATTALIONS	PREVIOUS TITLE (1903)	19TH CENTURY TITLE
1st Battalion	73rd Carnatic Infantry	13th Madras Infantry
2nd Battalion	75th Carnatic Infantry	15th Madras Infantry
3rd Battalion*	79th Carnatic Infantry	19th Madras Infantry
4th Battalion**	83rd Wallajahbad Light	23rd (Wallajahbad)
10th Training	Infantry	Madras Light Infantry
Battalion***	86th Carnatic Infantry	26th Madras Infantry
*disbanded in November 1923 **disbanded in June 1923 ***disbanded in May 1926		

The five regular battalions of the regiment found their origins in the old Madras army.

The 1st was raised as 13th Carnatic Infantry – 1776,
The 2nd was raised as 15th Carnatic Infantry – 1776,
The 3rd was raised as 20th Carnatic Infantry – 1777,
The 4th was raised as 33rd Madras Native Infantry – 1794,
The 5th was raised as 36th Madras Native Infantry – 1794.

All of them took part in the wars against Mysore and in the Burmese Expeditions. The 3rd was the only one involved in the Mutiny's suppression.

First World War
All battalions served in Mesopotamia. Their main tasks were limited to protecting communications. After 1918, the Kurd rebellion gave them the opportunity to show their value.

3rd Battalion fought well during the third Afghan War.
Between 1923 and 1928, all battalions were successively disbanded.
The regiment was only reformed in 1941 by the addition of the territorial Battalions.

Second World War

Wartime-raised units
1st Battalion (ex. 11th Territorial) took part in the war in Burma and in peacekeeping operations in Indonesia.
2nd Battalion (ex. 12th Territorial) went to Malaya. In January 1947, the battalion received airborne training and joined 2nd Indian Airborne Division.
3rd Battalion (ex. 13th Territorial) became a cadre battalion for the training of VCO's and NCO's.
4th Battalion (ex. 15th Territorial) was the first battalion to see action in Burma.
5th, 6th and 7th Battalions were raised and carried on the traditions of 63rd Palamcottah LI, 80th Carnatic and 88th Carnatic.
The 25th, 26th, 27th and 28th Battalions were disbanded in 1946.

Partition
In August 1947, 1st, 2nd, 3rd and 4th Battalions were allotted to India.
Last dress uniform
Scarlet, emerald green facings.
Class composition (1940)
Madrassi.

Battle Honours
Amboor, Carnatic, Sholinghur, Mysore, Seringapatam, Assaye, Cochin, Bourbon, Seetabuldee, Nagpore, Maheidpoor, Kernmendine, Ava, China 1840-42, Pegu, Lucknow, Central India, Afghanistan 1879-80, Burma 1885-87, Malakand, Tirah, Punjab, Frontier, China 1900, Afghanistan 1919.
Kut-al-Amara, Baghdad, Mesopotamia 1915-18, Aden, Persia 1918, NW Frontier India 1914-15, 1917, Baluchistan 1918, Kilimanjaro, East Africa 1914-16.
Tamu Road, Ukhrul, Ava, Kama, Burma 1942-45.

The 4th Bombay Grenadiers

BATTALIONS	PREVIOUS TITLE (1903)	19TH CENTURY TITLE
1st Battalion	101st Grenadiers	1st Bombay Grenadiers
2nd Battalion	102nd Prince of Wales's	2nd Prince of Wales's Own
3rd Battalion*	Own Grenadiers	Bombay Grenadiers
4th Battalion*	108th Infantry	8th Bombay Infantry
5th Battalion**	109th Infantry	9th Bombay Infantry
10th Training	112th Infantry	12th Bombay Infantry
Battalion***	113th Infantry	13th Bombay Infantry

*disbanded in 1930   **disbanded in 1933
***merged with the 10/9th Jat in 1929 to form a common training centre for both
   regiments

8th Bombay Native Infantry was raised in 1779. It was part of the Mangalore Garrison which capitulated to the 150,000-strong Mysore army after an eight month siege. In recognition of its brilliant conduct, the regiment was awarded the title "Grenadier".

2nd Battalion was raised in Calicut in 1796 as 13th Bombay Native Infantry. In 1798, the 8th and 13th BNI became 1st and 2nd Battalion of 1st Bombay Infantry, respectively. 10th Battalion, raised in 1800, took part in the Egypt expedition with 2nd Battalion.

During the following years, the battalions were in action to restrain the Mahratta princes within their own territory. In 1818, 2nd Battalion also won the title "Grenadier" after defeating 20,500 Mahrattas with the help of 300 cavalrymen from the Poona Horse.

In 1821, 10th Battalion went on to the coast of Arabia to campaign against the pirates. All battalions were in action in the Sind, Hyderabad and South Punjab. In 1880, 1st Battalion fought a stubborn defensive action in Kandahar. Further campaigns of the regiment were Burma, Aden and Somalia.

First World War
The 1st served in East Africa, Egypt and Palestine. The 2nd landed in Muscat and participated in the attempt to break the encirclement of Kut-el-Amara. Two of its companies were decimated in this action. The 10th fought in Mesopotamia at Sharqat and garrisoned in Aden.

Second World War
The 1st Battalion fought mainly in the Near East (Iran, Iraq, Egypt, Lebanon, and Syria). The 2nd was involved in the Burma and Malaya campaigns.

Wartime-raised units:
the 3rd, raised again in 1940, served in Burma;

the 4th, raised again in 1941, served in Burma and Iraq;

the 5th, raised again in 1941, served in Burma and was disbanded in 1946;

the 6th, raised in July 1942, had only a ten-month life;

the 11th (territorial) became 1st Battalion of the Ajmer Regiment;

a 25th (Garrison) Battalion was raised in 1941, as well as a 27th which became 2nd Battalion of the Ajmer Regiment in 1942.

Partition
The 1st, 2nd, 3rd and 4th and 25th Battalions were allotted to the Indian Army.
Last dress uniform
Scarlet, white facings.
Class composition (1940)
Jats, Punjabi Muslims.

Battle Honours
Mangalore, Mysore, Seringapatam, Egypt 1801, Kirkee, Corygaum, Beni Boo Ali, Meeanee, Hyderabad, Mooltan, Punjaub, Central India, Abyssinia, Kandahar 1880, Afghanistan 1878-80, Burma 1885-87, Somaliland 1902-04,
Egypt 1916-17, Gaza, Megiddo, Nablus, Palestine 1917-18, Aden, Tigris 1916, Kut-al-Arnara 1917, Baghdad, Sharqat, Mesopotamia 1915-18, East Africa 1914-16, Afghanistan 1919.
Kohima, Kalewa, Capture of Meiktila, Defence of Meiktila, Fort Dufferin Taungtha, Pegu 1945, Burma 1942-45.

4th Grenadiers, 1895, 1908 and 1942. (Artwork by Mike Chappell)

5th Mahratta Light Infantry

BATTALIONS	PREVIOUS TITLE (1903)	19TH CENTURY TITLE
1st Battalion	103rd Mahratta Light Infantry	3rd Bombay Light Infantry
2nd Battalion	105th Mahratta Light Infantry	5th Bombay Light Infantry
3rd Battalion	110th Mahratta Light Infantry	10th Bombay Light Infantry
4th Battalion	116th Mahrattas	16th Bombay Infantry
5th Battalion (Royal)	117th Mahrattas	17th Bombay Infantry
10th Training Battalion	114th Mahrattas	14th Bombay Infantry

Mahratta Light Infantry was formed in 1768 when the Company was forced to organise protective defence of the island of Bombay. This resulted in the creation of 2nd Bombay Sepoys, later 103rd Mahratta LI and the present 1st Battalion. 2nd Battalion was raised in 1788. From their foundation, both battalions were continuously employed in operations on the Bombay mainland and in central India. The 2nd was present at the capture of Colombo in 1796.

In 1797, the Travancore Regiment of Bombay NI was created to become 3rd Battalion. The two former battalions played a distinguished part in the extinction of Tipu Sahib and in the capture of Seringapatam. In 1800, units were raised which later became the 4th, 5th and 10th Battalions.

The six battalions took part in the campaigns against the Mahrattas, the Pindaris and the irregular plunderers of central India. In 1819, 1st and 2nd Battalions were engaged against the Arabian pirates. 1st Battalion suffered heavy losses when overwhelmed by the formidable Beni Boo Ali.

During the first Afghan War, 2nd Battalion won the Kahun honour for the defence of the fort that bears the same name. The 1/5th fought against the Sikhs in Multan and Gujerat. All battalions were employed in the suppression of rebellion in central India in 1857. 1st and 3rd Battalions were in Abyssinia in 1867. The 2nd, 3rd and 4th fought in the second Afghan War of 1879. 5th Mahratta Light Infantry units also went to Burma and East Africa.

First World War

1st, 3rd and 5th Battalions formed part of the original expeditionary force to the Persian Gulf in 1914. They fought in Kut and Ctesiphon and were subsequently captured in Kut. The 114th Mahrattas (10th Battalion) were lucky enough to participate in the final stage of the war in Mesopotamia. The 2nd and 4th Battalions earned honours in Palestine.

The 5th (reconstituted) went to Persia where it stayed until 1920, while the 1st and 3rd, back from captivity and having been reinforced, served during the third Afghan War and in North West Frontier operations. The 2nd sailed to Burma in 1931 to fight a local rebellion.

Second World War

The 1st Battalion served in Iraq, Egypt and Italy. In September 1945, it was needed for service with 268th Brigade which went to Japan for occupational duties. 2nd Battalion went to Italian East Africa and Egypt, was lost at Tobruk and raised again in 1946 from the 18th Battalion. 3rd Battalion was also sent to East Africa and Egypt and was designated for conversion to a parachute role in 1946. 4th Battalion fought in Burma and in Indonesia. 5th Battalion served in Persia and Egypt.

Wartime-raised units: fifteen additional battalions were formed:

the 6th fought in Burma, Dutch India and Malaya;

the 7th, 8th and 9th were converted to anti-tank artillery;

the 11th and 12th Territorials took the numbers 15th and 16th.

Partition

The regiment (1st, 2nd, 3rd, 4th and 5th Battalions) was allotted to India.

Last dress uniform

Scarlet, black facings.

Class composition (1940)

Mahrattas.

Battle Honours

Mysore, Seedaseer, Beni Boo Ali, Seringapatarn, Mooltan, Kahun, Gujerat, Punjab, Central India, China 1860-62, Abyssinia, Afghanistan 1879-80, Burma 1885-87, British East Africa 1901. Basra, Ctesiphon, Kut-al-Amara, Defence of Kut-al-Amara. Baghdad, Sharqat, Mesopotamia 1914-18, Persia 1918, Megiddo, Nablus, Sharon. Tobruk 1941, Keren, Gobi II, Tobruk 1942, The Sangro, Tengnoupal, Sangshak, Burma 1942-45. Advance to Florence, Gothic Line, Ruywa, The Senio Italy 1943-45.

6th Rajputana Rifles

BATTALIONS	PREVIOUS TITLE (1903)	19TH CENTURY TITLE
1st Battalion	104th Wellesley's Rifles	4th Bombay Rifles
2nd Battalion	120th Rajputana Infantry	20th Bombay Infantry
3rd Battalion	122nd Rajputana Infantry	22nd Bombay Infantry
4th Battalion	123rd Outram's Rifles	23rd Bombay Rifles
5th Battalion	125th Napier's Rifles	25th Bombay Rifles
10th Training Battalion	13th Rajput (the Shekhawati) Regiment	13th (Shekhawati) Rajput Infantry

The story of 1st Battalion begins in 1775. The formation was immediately in action in Deccan and participated in Wellesley's campaigns in central India. The 1/6th distinguished itself in Multan (1848) before going to Persia and participating in the Mutiny's suppression. The battalion fought in Kandahar and took part in the Somalia expedition.

2nd and 3rd Battalions were raised in 1817 and in 1818. The 2nd served in Sind, in the Afghan War and in Persia. The 3rd had to wait until 1900 before gaining its first honour in China.

4th and 5th Battalions were raised after the Battle of Kirkee. The 4th fought the first Afghan War and participated in fighting the guerrillas of Burma (1885). The 5th saw action in Sind and was present at the capture of Gwalior during the Mutiny. It also participated in the expedition in Abyssinia.

While the first five battalions originated from the Bombay army, the 10th was created in Bengal. Its ancestor unit is a police force created in Jodhpur to control the turbulent Shekhawati tribe. The 10th fought at Aliwal and was one of the Bengal Regiments remaining loyal during the Mutiny.

First World War

The first two battalions were captured at Kut. Reconstituted in 1917, they served in the Middle East. The 3rd saw little action in Iraq. The 4th was in Allenby's victorious advance into Jerusalem. The 5th was integrated into 3rd Lahore Division which fought in France. Later, they were part of 7th Meerut Division in Mesopotamia.

After the War, Napier's Rifles were despatched to Waziristan to conduct pacification activities against the rebel tribes.

Second World War

1st Battalion (Wellesley's) fought in Italian East Africa, Egypt and Italy. The 2nd (POW) served in the Middle East. The 3rd participated in the Burma campaign. The 4th (Outram's) went along with the 1st Battalion until its conversion to an airborne formation in 1944. The 5th (Napier's) participated in the campaigns of Burma, Malaya and the Dutch Indies.

Wartime-raised units: eleven battalions were raised. The 7th Battalion was taken prisoner in Singapore in February 1941.

Partition
The first five battalions were allotted to the Indian Army.
Last dress uniform
Rifle green, red facings.
Class composition (1940)
Jats, Punjabi Muslims, Rajput.

Battle Honours
Mysore, Seringapatam, Bourbon, Kirkee, Beni Boo Ali, Meeanee, Hyderabad, Aliwal, Mooltan, Punjab, Reshire, Bushire, Khooshab, Persia, Central India, Abyssinia, Kandahar 1880, Chitral, Afghanistan 1879-80, Burma, 1885-87, British East Africa1898, China 1900, Afghanistan 1919, Givenchy 1914-, Neuve Chapelle, Aubers, Festubert 1915, France and Flanders 1915-15, Egypt 1915, Gaza, Nebi Samwil, Jerusalem, Tell Asur, Megiddo, Sharon, Sharon, Palestine 1917-18, Basra, Shaiba, Kut-al-Amara 1915-17, Ctesiphon, Defence of Kut-al-Amara, Tigris 1916, Baghdad, Mesopotamia 1914-18, Persia 1918, East Africa 1914, Agordat, Barentu, Keren, Abyssinia 1940-41, Derna, Damascus 1941, Deir-es-Zor, Kissoue, Raqaa, Sidi Barrani, Omars, Gubi II, Alem Harnza, Benghazi, Carmusa, Gazala, The Cauldron, The Kennels, Mersa Matruh, Ruweisat Ridge, Alam el Halfa, El Alamein, Mareth, Djebel el Meida, Djebel Garci, Enfidaville, Tunis North Africa 1940-43, Cassino I, Monastery Hill, Hangman's Hill, Transimene Line, Montone, Citta di Castello, Pian di Magio, Monte Calvo, Italy 1943-45, Johore, The Muar, Singapore Island, Malaya 1941-42, Rathedaung, Htizwe, Imphal, Shenam Pass, Litan, Ukhrul, Tengnoupal, Kyaukmyaung Bridgehead, Mandalay, Fort Dufferin, Meiktila, Maymyo, Pyinrnana, Toungoo, Burma 1942-45.

6th Rajputana Rifles, 1912, 1918 and 1930. (Artwork by Mike Chappell)

The 7th Rajput Regiment

BATTALIONS	PREVIOUS TITLE (1903)	19TH CENTURY TITLE
1st Battalion	2nd Queen's Own Rajput	2nd (Queen's Own) Rajput
2nd Battalion	Light Infantry	Light Infantry
3rd Battalion	4th Prince Albert Victor's	4th (Prince Albert Victor's)
4th Battalion	Rajput	Rajput Infantry
5th Battalion	7th Duke of Connaught's	7th (Duke of Connaught's
10th Training	Own Rajput	Own) Rajput Infantry
Battalion	8th Rajput	8th Rajput Infantry
	11th Rajput	11th Rajput Infantry
	16th Rajput Regiment (The	15th (Lucknow) Rajput
	Lucknow Regiment)	Infantry

1st, 2nd, 3rd and 4th Battalions were raised in 1798. The 1st and 2nd were part of Lord Lake's army which defeated the Mahratta princes and put an end to French ambitions in northern India at the battle of Leswarree. In recognition of its distinguished conduct, 1st QO Battalion was granted a special standard bearing the words "Lake and Victory".

5th Battalion was created in 1825. During the Mutiny, 2nd and 4th Battalions were disarmed but were immediately rearmed and sent to Punjab. The 10th was composed of loyal elements of three other Bengal units and named the Lucknow Regiment.

After the Mutiny, most battalions were continuously in action:

In China 1858-59 – 3rd and 5th Battalions,

In Afghanistan 1878-1880 – 1st, 2nd, 5th and 10th Battalions,

In Egypt 1882 – 3rd Battalion,

In Burma 1885-1887 – 1st, 2nd, 5th and 10th Battalions,

In China 1900 – 1st and 3rd Battalions.

First World War

All battalions served in Mesopotamia.

Second World War

The 1st and 2nd served in Burma. The 3rd fought in Egypt and, in 1946, it was integrated into 77th Para Brigade. The 4th served in Egypt. The 5th was captured in Hong-Kong in 1941.

Wartime-raised units: ten additional battalions were raised. The 14th, born from 12th Territorial, became regular in 1941.

Partition

The regiment went to the Indian Army (1st, 2nd, 3rd, 4th and 14th Battalions)

Last dress uniform

Scarlet, yellow facings.

Class composition (1940)

Punjabi Muslims, Rajput.

Battle Honours

Delhi 1803, Leswarree, Deig, Bhurtpore, Afghanistan 1839, Khelat, Cabool 1842, Maharajpore, Moodkee, Ferozeshah, Aliwal, Sobraon, Chillianwallah, Goojerat, Punjaub, Lucknow, Central India, China 1858-59, Afghanistan 1878-80, Tel-el-Kebir, Egypt 1882, Burma 1885-87, Pekin 1900, China 1900, Macedonia 1918, Suez Canal, Egypt 1915, Aden, Basra, Kut-al-Amara 1915, Ctesiphon, Defence of Kut-al-Amara, Tigris 1916, Mesopotamia 1914-18, Persia 1915-18, NW Frontier India 1915, 1917, Afghanistan 1919, Hong Kong, South East Asia 1941-42, El Alamein, North Africa 1940-41, Donbaik, Razabil, Point 551, Ngakyedauk Pass, Imphal, Tiddim Road, Kohima, Relief of Kohima, Meiktila, Capture of Meiktila, Defence of Meiktila, Taungtha, Rangoon Road, Sittang 1945, Burma 1942-45.

7th Rajputs, 1910, 1911 and 1937. (Artwork by Mike Chappell)

8th Punjab Regiment

BATTALIONS	PREVIOUS TITLE (1903)	19TH CENTURY TITLE
1st Battalion	1/89th Punjabis (1914)	29th Burma Infantry
2nd Battalion	90th Punjabis	30th Burma Infantry
3rd Battalion	91st Punjabis	31st Burma Light Infantry
4th Battalion	92nd Punjabis	32nd Burma Infantry
5th Battalion	93rd Punjabis	33rd Burma Infantry
10th Training Battalion	2/89th Punjabis	29th Burma Infantry

The origin of 8th Regiment can be traced through the Old Madras Army. In 1893, 19th, 30th, 31st, 32nd and 33rd Madras Infantry were made up of Sikhs and Punjabis and renamed "Burma Infantry".

It may be said that the Afghan campaign of 1878-1880 and the service on the North West Frontier set the seal on the future of Madras soldiers. They suffered so much from the extremes of cold that it questioned their ability for service in the troubled mountain spots. Until 1883, the Madras Battalions had mainly served in Burma.

In 1900, the 31st participated in the China expedition.

First World War

During the War, the men of 1st Battalion served in more theatres as did any other unit of the British Empire armies.

While on their way to Egypt, they landed to destroy the Turkish fort of Turba on the Red Sea.

They defended the Suez Canal, before arriving on the Gallipoli Peninsula. Within less than a month, they were sent on to France as reinforcements for 3rd Lahore Division into the Loos sector.

Withdrawn with the Indian Corps, they went to Mesopotamia. After serving on the North West Frontier in India, they were sent back to Mesopotamia again and ended the war in Salonika.

Their wanderings were not over yet and for the next few years, they marched all over Caucasia until the politicians decided on their attitude towards the Bolsheviks.

The 2/8th served in Mesopotamia and took part in the third Afghan War. The 3rd and the 4th Battalions participated in the final victories in Mesopotamia and in Palestine. The 5th was with the 1st in the Suez Canal zone. They reinforced the Meerut Division in France and spent the last two years of the war in Egypt and in Mesopotamia.

Second World War

The 1st Battalion was captured in Singapore.

The 2nd Battalion fought in Burma.

The 3rd was in Egypt and in Italy.

The 4th served in Iraq and in Iran.

The 5th campaigned in Burma, in Malaya and spent the last days of the war in Indonesia.

Wartime raised units:

The 6th Battalion was raised in 1940 and fought in Burma;

The 7th Battalion was captured in Singapore;

The 8th Battalion served in Burma;

The 9th Battalion was re-named 1/8th in 1946;

The 14th, 15th, 16th, 25th and 26th Battalions remained in India for the duration of the war.

Partition
The 8th Punjab was allotted to Pakistan.
Last dress uniform
Khaki, dark blue facings.
Class composition (1940)
Gujaris, Punjabi Muslims, Sikhs.

Battle Honours
Cochin, Maheidpore, Ava, Afghanistan 1878-80, Burma 1885-87, China 1900, Loos, France and Flanders 1915, Macedonia 1918, Helles, Krithia, Gallipoli 1915, Suez Canal, Egypt 1915, Megiddo, Sharon, Palestine 1918, Tigris 1916, Kut-al-Amara 1917, Baghdad, Khan Baghdadi, Mesopotamia 1915-18, Afghanistan 1919.
North Malaya, Jitra, Gurun, Malaya 1941-42, The Trigno, Perano, The Sangro, Villa Grande, Gustav Line, Monte Grande, The Senio, Italy 1943-45, Donbaik, North Arakan, The Shweli, Myitson, Kama, Burma 1942-45.

8th Punjabis, 1903, 1918 and 1930. (Artwork by Mike Chappell)

9th Jat Regiment

BATTALIONS	PREVIOUS TITLE (1903)	19TH CENTURY TITLE
1st Battalion (Royal)	1/6th Jat Light Infantry (1914)	6th Jat Light Infantry
2nd Battalion	119th Infantry (the Mooltan	14th Bombay Infantry
3rd Battalion	Regiment)	10th Jat Infantry
4th Battalion	10th Jats	18th Musulman Rajput
10th Training Battalion	18th Infantry	Infantry
	2/6th Jat Light Infantry (1914)	6th Jat Light Infantry

1st Battalion was raised in 1803 under the name of 1st Battalion/22nd BNI. It first saw action in the battle of Nagpur in 1817. 2nd Battalion was born in the Bombay army as 1st Battalion/10th Bombay Infantry. 3rd Battalion was created due to troubles in Burma in 1823. It was then named 1/33rd Bengal Infantry. 1st and the 2nd Battalions were engaged in the first Afghan War and the two Sikh Wars.

1st and the 3rd Battalions were not affected during the Mutiny. After the suppression of the rebellion, 3rd Battalion went to China to take part in the Opium War. During the second Afghan War, the 1st Battalion distinguished itself at Ali Masjid while the 2nd Battalion besieged Kandahar. The 3rd Battalion went again to Burma from 1888 until 1890. The 1st sailed to China to participate in the Boxer War of 1900.

First World War

The 1/9th fought in France (Dehra Dun Brigade – Meerut Division) before being sent to Kut to relieve the 2/9th which was besieged. The 3/9th acted mainly as a reinforcement reserve for the 1st and the 2nd.

After the war, the three battalions were mainly engaged on the North West Frontier. The 4/9th were kept in garrison in Hong-Kong and China.

Second World War

2nd and 4th Regular Battalions were captured in Singapore by the Japanese. 1st Battalion saw action in Burma, Thailand and Malaysia. 3rd Battalion went to the Middle East and Egypt before joining the army in Burma.

Wartime-raised units:

5th and 6th Battalions, raised in 1941, participated in the fights in Burma and became regular after the war;

7th (ex.11th Territorial) was also in Burma;

8th (ex. 12th Territorial) remained in India with 9th, 14th, 26th and 27th Battalions;

15th took the 2nd Battalion number in 1946 to replace the unit captured by the Japanese.

The "Kumaon Rifles"

In October 1917, the Kumaoni were enrolled to form 4/39th Garhwal Rifles. One month later, they became 4/39th Kumaon Rifles. In April 1918, the name was changed again to 1/50th Kumaon Rifles. The battalion fought gallantly in Palestine under that name.

When the war ended, the 1/50th were despatched to Istanbul to join the Black Sea Army. The unit was not disbanded in 1918 and was attached to 9th Jat without becoming an organic unit within the regiment.

Partition
The regiment was allotted to the Indian Army (1st, 2nd, 3rd, 5th and 6th Battalions).
Last dress uniform
Scarlet, blue facings.
Class composition (1940)
Jats, Rajput Muslims, Punjabi Muslims.

The "Kumaon Rifles"
Last dress uniform
Dark green, black facings.
Class composition (1940)
Kumaoni.

Battle Honours
Nagpur, Afghanistan 1839, Ghuznee 1839, Candahar 1842, Ghuznee 1842, Cabool 1842, Maharajpore, Sobraon, Mooltan, Goojerat, Punjab, Ali Masjid, China 1858-62, Kandahar 1880, Afghanistan 1879-80, Burma 1885-87, China 1900 La Bassee 1914, Festubert 1914-15, Neuve Chapelle, France and Flanders 1914-15, Shaiba, Defence of Kut-al-Amara, Ctesiphon, Tigris 1916, Khan Baghdadi, Mesopotamia 1914-18, Kut-al-Amara 1915, NW Frontier, India 1914-15, 1917, Afghanistan 1919, Razabil, Kanglatongbi, Kampar, Malaya 1941-42, Burma 1942-45, Nungshigum, Jitra, The Muar, North Africa 1940-43.

The 9th Jats, 1870, 1895 and 1930. (Artwork by Mike Chappell)

10th Baluch Regiment

BATTALIONS	PREVIOUS TITLE (1903)	19TH CENTURY TITLE
1st Battalion	1/124th (Duchess of Connaught's	24th (Duchess of Connaught's
2nd Battalion	Own) Baluchistan Infantry	Own) Baluchistan Infantry
3rd Battalion	126th Baluchistan Infantry	26th Baluchistan Infantry
4th Battalion	127th Baluch Light Infantry	27th Baluch Light Infantry
5th Battalion	129th (Duke of Connaught's Own)	29th (Duke of Connaught's Own)
10th Training	Baluchis	Baluch Infantry
Battalion	130th Baluchis	30th Baluch Infantry
	2/124th (Duchess of Connaught's	24th (Duchess of Connaught's
	Own) Baluchistan Infantry	Own) Baluchistan Infantry

1st Battalion of 10th Regiment originated in 2nd (Marine) Battalion of 13th Bombay Infantry Regiment raised in 1820, and immediately engaged in the Persian Gulf operations. 2nd Battalion was raised in 1825. 3rd and the 4th Battalions were formed in 1844 and 1846 respectively.

2nd and 4th Battalions fought together at Kushab during the 1856-1857 war against Persia. 3rd Battalion was part of the force which captured Delhi and pacified Hindustan after the Mutiny. The 3rd went also to Abyssinia in 1867. 1st, 3rd, 4th and 5th Battalions participated in the second Afghan War.

During the years that followed,

> 4th Battalion went to Egypt in 1882,
>
> 3rd Battalion was engaged in Upper Burma in 1886,
>
> 1st and 3rd Battalions sailed to East Africa in 1896,
>
> 2nd and 5th Battalions joined the International Force to put down the Boxers in 1900,
>
> 3rd Battalion went to Somalia again in 1909.

First World War

The Western Front honours were all earned by the 4th Battalion (3rd Division). The other battalions were engaged in Mesopotamia and East Africa. The 1st and 4th Battalions participated in the third Afghan War.

Second World War

The battalions were present in several theatres of operation:

> 1st Battalion: Iraq, Iran, Syria, Egypt;
>
> 2nd Battalion: Malaya – captured in Singapore in 1942;
>
> 3rd Battalion: Iraq, Iran, Egypt, Sicily, Italy – converted to a parachute battalion;
>
> 4th Battalion: East Africa, Egypt, Cyprus, Italy;
>
> 5th Battalion: Burma.

Wartime-raised units: nine additional battalions were raised between 1940 and 1942:

> 7th, 8th, 14th and 16th fought in Burma;
>
> 17th was present in Iraq, Palestine, Greece and Libya;
>
> 7th became regular in 1945;
>
> the 9th replaced the 2nd after its capture.

Partition
The regiment went to the Pakistan army.
Last dress uniform
Green, red trousers, cherry facings.
Class composition (1940)
Dogras, Pathans, Punjabi Muslims, Sikhs.

Battle Honours
Aden, Reshire, Bushire, Koosh-ab, Persia. Delhi 1857, Central India, Abyssinia, Kandahar 1880, Afghanistan 1878-80, Egypt 1882, Tel-el-Kebir, Burmah 1885-87, British East Africa 1896, British East Africa 1897-99, China 1900, Messines 1914, Armentieres 1914, Ypres 1914-15, Gheluvelt, Festubert 1914, Givenchy 1914, Neuve Chapelle, St Julien, France and Flanders 1914-15, Egypt 1915, Megiddo, Sharon, Palestine 1918, Aden, Kut-al-Amara 1917, Baghdad, Mesopotamia 1916-18, Persia 1915-18, NW Frontier, India 1917, Kilimanjaro, Behobeho, East Africa 1915-18, Afghanistan 1919. Gallabat, Barentu, Massawa, The Cauldron, Ruweisat Ridge, El Alamein, North Africa 1940-43, Landing in Sicily, Sicily 1943, Castel Frentano, Orsogna, Arezzo, Monte Cedrone, Citta di Castello, Monte Calvo, Gothic Line, Plan di Castello, Croce, Gemmano Ridge, San Marino, San Paulo-Monte Spacata, Monte Cavallo, Cesena, Savio Bridgehead, Casa Bettini, Idice Bridgehead, Italy 1943-45, Athens, Greece 1944-45, North Malaya, Machang, Singapore Island, Malaya 1941-42, Kuzeik, North Arkan, Point 551, Maungdaw, Shwebo, Kyaukmyaung Bridgehead, Mandalay, Capture of Meiktila, Defence of Meiktila, The Irrawaddy, Pegu 1945, Sittang 1945, Burma 1942-45.

10th Baluchs, 1913, 1915 and 1918. (Artwork by Mike Chappell)

11th Sikh Regiment

BATTALIONS	PREVIOUS TITLE (1903)	19TH CENTURY TITLE
1st Battalion	14th Ferozepore Sikhs	14th (Ferozepore) Sikh Infantry
2nd Battalion	15th Ludhiana Sikhs	15th (Ludhiana) Sikh Infantry
3rd Battalion	45th Rattray's Sikhs	45th (Rattray's) Sikh Infantry
4th Battalion	36th Sikhs	36th Sikh Infantry
5th Battalion	47th Sikhs	47th Sikh Infantry
10th Training Battalion	35th Sikhs	35th Sikh Infantry

The first two Sikh units were raised in 1846. From the beginning, the Sikh Regiments integrated Punjabi Muslims. The Ferozepore Regiment gained fame during the Mutiny. In 1855, Captain T. Rattray had created a police unit which became the 3/11th. Because of the Russian threat, 4th and 10th Battalions were raised in 1887. The 5th was formed in 1901.

The battalions of the Sikh Regiment participated in the wars in Afghanistan and China (1860 and 1900). The 4th won the "Samana" honour when 19 sepoys and two cooks defended Samana fort for six hours against thousands of fanatic tribesmen. All defenders were killed while gaining this unique honour for their battalion.

First World War

The 1st Battalion suffered heavy losses in Gallipoli. 2nd and 5th Battalions fought in France (7th Division). 3rd and 4th Battalions were in Mesopotamia. 2nd and 10th Battalions were engaged in the Afghan War of 1919. 3rd Battalion fought with distinction during the Arab rebellion in Iraq while 1st Battalion was airlifted to Kurk during the Kurd uprising of 1923.

Second World War

11th Sikh Regiment were engaged on different fronts:

1st Battalion took part in the Burma operations;

2nd Battalion served in Iraq, Iran, Egypt, Cyprus, Italy and Greece;

3rd Battalion went to Iraq, Iran and Lebanon;

4th Battalion rejoined Italy in 1945 with the 10th Division;

5th Battalion was captured in Singapore in 1942.

Wartime-raised units: nine additional battalions were raised and remained in India except for the Machine-Gun Battalion which went to Burma and 7th Battalion which served in the Middle East and became regular in 1945.

Partition

The regiment was allotted to India (1st, 2nd, 3rd, 4th and 7th Battalions).

Last dress uniform

Scarlet, yellow facings, except the 2nd Battalion (Emerald green facings) and the 3rd Battalion (White facings).

Class composition (1940)

Punjabi Muslims, Sikhs.

Battle Honours

Defence of Arrah, Lucknow, Behar, China 1860-62, Ali Masjid, Ahmed Khel, Kandahar 1880, Afghanistan 1878-80, Tofrek, Suakin 1885, Defence of Chitral, Chitral, Malakand, Punjab Frontier, Samana, Tirah, China 1900.

La Bassee 1914, Armentieres 1914, Givenchy 1914, Neuve Chapelle, Ypres 1915, St Julien, Aubers, Festubert 1915, France and Flanders 1914-15, Helles, Krithia, Suvla, Sari Bair-, Gallipoli 1915, Suez Canal, Egypt 1915-16, Megiddo, Sharon, Palestine 1918, Tigris 1916, Kut-al-Amara 1917, Baghdad, Sharqat, Mesopotamia 1916-18, Persia 1918, NW Frontier, India 1914, 1915, 1916-17, Tsingtao, Afghanistan 1919.

Agordat, Keren, Abyssinia 1940-41, Iraq 1941, Omars, Mersa Matruh, Deir el Shein, North Africa 1940-43, Gothic Line, Monte Calvo, Coriano, Poggio San Giovanni, San Marino, Italy 1943-45, Greece 1944-45, Kuantan, Niyor, Malaya 1941-42, North Arakan, Buthidaung, Kanglatongbi, Nyaungu Bridgehead, The Irrawaddy 1945, Shandatgyi, Kama, Sittang 1945, Burma 1942-45.

11th Sikhs, 1900 and 1945. (Artwork by Mike Chappell)

12th Frontier Force Regiment

BATTALIONS	PREVIOUS TITLE (1903)	19TH CENTURY TITLE
1st Battalion	51st Sikhs (Frontier Force)	1st Sikh Infantry
2nd Battalion	52nd Sikhs (Frontier Force)	2nd (Hill) Sikh Infantry
3rd Battalion	53rd Sikhs (Frontier Force)	3rd Sikh Infantry
(Royal)	54th Sikhs (Frontier Force)	4th Sikh Infantry
4th Battalion	1st Battalion Queen Victoria's Own	Queen's Own Corps of
5th Battalion	Corps of Guides (Frontier Force)	Guides
10th Training	(Lumsden's)	Queen's Own Corps of
Battalion	2nd Battalion Queen Victoria's Own	Guides
	Corps of Guides (Frontier Force)	
	(Lumsden's)	

The regiment was raised from the Police and created to keep order in the territory crossed by the Sutlej River (Punjab). The first four battalions found their roots in the Frontier Brigade of 1846. The 5th and 10th came from the Corps of Guides Infantry.

The battalions of the Frontier Brigade were not single-class. They were a mix of different classes such as Sikhs, Dogras, Pathans, Punjabi Muslims and even Gurkhas. In 1815, the Sikh regiments were integrated into the Punjab Irregular Force and the acronym "PIF" entered the Indian Military vocabulary. In 1842, the 4th Battalion volunteered for Burma. All units took part in the suppression of the Mutiny.

The Guides became Queen's Own in 1876 and fought in the second Afghan War along with 1st, 2nd and 3rd Battalions

First World War

All battalions served in Egypt and in the Middle East.

In the interwar period, the regiment was active on the North West Frontier.

Second World War

The 1st Battalion campaigned in Iraq, Syria and Italy with 17th Brigade/8th Division. In 1946, it became a parachute battalion of 2nd Division. 2nd Battalion was captured by the Japanese in Singapore. 3rd Battalion wandered in East Africa, Egypt and Iraq. After a training period in Cyprus, they fought in Italy and Sicily before ending the war in Greece. The 4th Battalion fought the first combats in Burma in 1942 (16th Brigade). 5th Battalion served in Iraq and Iran.

Wartime-raised units: nine additional battalions were raised between 1940 and 1942:

the 8th, 9th, 14th and the "Machine-Gun" Battalion participated in the war in Burma;

1st "Afridi" Battalion served in the Middle East;

9th Battalion was re-named 2/12th.

Partition
The regiment was allotted to the Pakistan army (1st, 2nd, 3rd, 4th, 5th and 8th Battalions).
Last dress uniform
Khaki, red facings.
Class composition (1940)
Dogras, Pathans, Punjabi Muslims, Sikhs.

Battle Honours
Pegu, Mooltan, Goojerat, Punjaub, Delhi 1857, Ali Masjid, Kabul 1879, Ahmed Khel, Kandahar 1880, Afghanistan 1878-80, Chitral, Malakand, Punjab Frontier, Tirah, Pekin 1900, Somaliland 1901-04.
Suez Canal, Egypt 1915, Megiddo, Sharon, Nablus, Palestine 1918, Aden, Tigris 1916, Kut-al-Amara 1917, Baghdad, Sharqat, Mesopotamia 1915-18, NW Frontier, India 1914, 1915, 1916-17, Afghanistan 1919.
Gallabat, Tehamiyam Wells, Agordat, Barentu, Keren, Amba Alagi, Abyssinia 1940-41, Gazala, Bir Hacheim, El Adem, North Africa 1940-43, Landing in Sicily, Sicily 1943, Landing at Reggio, The Sangro, Mozzagrogna, Romagnoli, The Moro, Impossible Bridge, Cassino II, Pignataro, Advance to Florence, Campriano, Gothic Line, Coriano, The Senio, Santerno Crossing, Italy 1943-45, Athens, Greece 1944-45, North Malaya, Kota Bharu, Central Malaya, Kuantan, Machang, Singapore Island, Malaya 1941-42, Moulmein, Sittang 1942, 1945, Pegu 1942, 1945, Taukkyan, Shwegyin, North Arakan, Buthidaung, Maungdaw, Ngakyedauk Pass, Imphal, Tamu Road, Shenam Pass, Bishenpur, Kyaukmyaung, Bridgehead, Arakan Beaches, Ramree, Taungup, Mandalay, Myinmu, Fort Dufferin, Kyaukse 1945, Meiktila, Nyaungu Bridgehead, Capture of Meiktila, Defence of Meiktila, The Irrawaddy, Rangoon Road, Pyawbwe, Toungoo, Burma 1942-45.

12th Frontier Force, 1910 and 1945. (Artwork by Mike Chappell)

13th Frontier Force Rifles

BATTALIONS	PREVIOUS TITLE (1903)	19TH CENTURY TITLE
1st Battalion	55th Coke's Rifles (Frontier Force)	1st Punjab Infantry
2nd Battalion	1/56th Punjabi Rifles (Frontier Force)	2nd Punjab Infantry
4th Battalion	57th Wilde's Rifles (Frontier Force)	4th Punjab Infantry
5th Battalion	58th Vaughan's Rifles (Frontier Force)	5th Punjab Infantry
6th Battalion (Royal)	59 Scinde Rifles (Frontier Force)	6th Punjab Infantry
10th Training Battalion	2/56th Punjabi Rifles (Frontier Force)	1st Punjab Infantry

In 1849, the 13th FF Rifles recruited the volunteer veterans of the Sikh Wars. In 1850, the Punjab Irregular Force (PIF) had a strength of:

5 Punjab Cavalry Regiments,

4 Mountain Artillery Batteries,

1 Garrison Artillery Battery,

4 Sikh Infantry Regiments,

6 Punjab Infantry Regiments,

1 Gurkha Regiment (the 5th FF).

During the Mutiny and the subsequent campaign, the PIF built their reputation upon loyalty, bravery and steadiness. Three Punjabi battalions were present at the siege of Delhi and two of them were part of the relief column to Lucknow.

In 1863, all battalions, except the 2nd, were campaigning on the North West Frontier. The PIF was actively involved in the second Afghan War. Their first overseas battle honour was earned by 4th Punjab which went to China in 1900.

In 1903, the five Punjab Infantry Regiments were renumbered in sequence from 55th to 59th. The 3rd had been disbanded before to save costs.

First World War

In 1914, the 57th and 59th were part of the Meerut Division in France and Mesopotamia. The 58th served with 7th Lahore Division in the same theatres. The 56th rejoined them in Mesopotamia. The 55th provided reinforcement to the other regiments. The first three regiments had raised a second battalion, but only the 2/56th remained active after the war.

In the interwar period, the regiment saw action mainly on the North West Frontier.

Second World War

1st Battalion: captured on Singapore Island in February 1942.

2nd Battalion: Burma, Dutch West Indies.

4th Battalion: Syria, Persia, Egypt, Italy.

5th Battalion: Iraq, Syria, Italy.

6th Battalion: Italian East Africa, Persia, Iraq, Syria, Palestine, Italy.

Wartime-raised units: eleven battalions were raised for the duration of the war. All were disbanded in 1946. The 14/13th was designated anew as 1/13th in 1946.

Partition
The regiment was allotted to Pakistan (1st, 2nd, 4th, 5th and 6th Battalions).
Last dress uniform
Rifle green, red facings.
Class composition (1940)
Dogras, Pathans, Punjabi Muslims, Sikhs.

Battle Honours
Delhi 1857, Lucknow, Peiwar Kotal, Charasiah, Kabul 1879, Afghanistan 1878-80, Tirah, Punjab Frontier, China 1900, La Bassee 1914, Messines 1914, Armentieres 1914, Festbubert 1914, 1915, Givenchy 1914-, Neuve Chapelle, Ypres 1915, St Julien, Aubers, Loos, France and Flanders 1914¬15, Suez Canal, Egypt 1915-17, Gaza, El Mughar, Nebi Samwil, Jerusalem, Megiddo, Sharon, Palestine 1917-18, Aden, Tigris 1917, Kut-al-Amara 1917, Baghdad, Mesopotamia 1916-18, Persia 1918-19, North-West Frontier, India 1917, Baluchistan 1918, East Africa 1916-18, Afghanistan 1919.
Gash Delta, Barentu, Keren, Ad Teclesan, Amba Alagi, Abyssinia 1940-41, Deir ez Zor, Raqaa, Syria 1941, Gazala, Sidi Rezegh 1942, Gambut, Mersa Matruh, North Africa 1940-43, The Trigno, Tufillo, The Sangro, Impossible Bridge, Villa Grande, Cassino II, Gustav Line, Pignataro, Advance to Florence, Gothic Line, Monte Grande, The Senio, Bologna, Monte Sole, Italy 1943-45, North Malaya, Kota Bharu, Johore, Gemas, The Muar, Singapore Island, Malaya 1941-42, Pegu 1942, Taukkyan, Monywa 1942, Shwegyin, North Arakan, Point 551, Mayu Tunnels, Maungdaw, Ngakyedauk Pass, Imphal, Litan, Arakan Beaches, Myebon, Ramree, Mandalay, Myinmu, Meiktila, Nyaungu Bridgehead, Capture of Meiktila, Defence of Meiktila, Taungtha, Myingyan, The Irrawaddy, Yenangyaung 1945, Magwe, Rangoon Road, Pegu 1945, Sittang 1945, Burma 1942-45.

13th Frontier Force, 1920, 1930 and 1945. (Artwork by Mike Chappell)

14th Punjab Regiment

BATTALIONS	PREVIOUS TITLE (1903)	19TH CENTURY TITLE
1st Battalion	19th Punjabis	19th Punjab Infantry
2nd Battalion	20th Duke of Cambridge 's Own	20th (Duke of Cambridge's
3th Battalion	Punjabis	Own) Punjab Infantry
4th Battalion	22nd Punjabis	22nd Punjab Infantry
5th Battalion	24th Punjabis	24th Punjab Infantry
10th Training Battalion	40th Pathans	40th Punjab Infantry
	21st Punjabis	21st Punjab Infantry

The regiment was made up of Punjabi units raised during the Mutiny and of Pathans from the Shalijchanpur Levy (40th). Despite service in Mutiny operations, the first battle honours were won in China in 1860 by 2nd and 3rd Battalions.

40th Pathans were the only Pathan Regiment in the Indian Army. They first saw action in Tibet in 1903-1904.

First World War

All battalions served in Egypt, Mesopotamia and Palestine. The 40th also fought in France with the Jullundur Brigade/3rd Division.

Second World War

No fewer than 17 battalions participated in the war.

With four battalions in the hands of the Japanese, the 14th had acquired an unfortunate reputation. The 1/14th, 5/14th and 16/14th were captured in Singapore and the 1/14th suffered the same fate in Hong-Kong. The 2nd was reconstituted by the 8/14th raised in 1941. Due to the large element of Jats present in these battalions, 11th and 12th Territorials became 9/9th Jat and 14/9th Jat. The 3rd, 4th, 7th and 9th Battalions fought in Burma.

Partition
The regiment was allotted to the Pakistan Army (1st, 2nd, 3rd and 4th Battalions).
Last dress uniform
Khaki, red facings.
Class composition (1940)
Pathans, Punjabi Muslims, Sikhs.

Battle Honours
Taku Forts, China 1860-62, Pekin 1860, Abyssinia, Ali Masjid, Ahmed Khel, Kandahar1880, Afghanistan 1878-80, Tel-el-Kebir, Egypt 1882, Punjab Frontier, Malakand, Pekin 1900, China 1900, Ypres 1915, St Julien, Aubers, France and Flanders 1915, Macedonia 1918, Suez Canal, Egypt 1915, Megiddo, Sharon, Nablus, Palestine 1918, Basra, Shaiba, Kut-al-Amara 1915, 1917, Ctesiphon, Defence of Kut-al-Amara, Baghdad, Khan Baghdadi, Mesopotamia 1914-18, Merv, Persia 1915-19, NW Frontier, India 1915-17, Narungombe, East Africa 1916-18, Afghanistan 1919, Agordat, Keren, Abyssinia 1940-41, Alam el Halfa, Defence of Alamein Line, North Africa 1940-43, Kampar, Singapore Island, Malaya 1941-42, Hong Kong, South East Asia 1941-42, The Yu, North Arakan, Buthidaung, Razabil, Maungdaw, Ngakyedauk Pass, Imphal, Shenam Pass, Nungshigum, Bishenpur, Kanglatongbi, Jessami, Naga Village, Mao Songsang, Monywa 1945, Kyaukse 1945, Nyaungu Bridgehead, Letse, Magwe, Rangoon Road, Pegu 1945, Sittang 1945, Burma 1942-45.

14th Punjabis, 1910 and 1941. (Artwork by Mike Chappell)

15th Punjab Regiment

BATTALIONS	PREVIOUS TITLE (1903)	19TH CENTURY TITLE
1st Battalion	25th Punjabis	25th Punjab Infantry
2nd Battalion	26th Punjabis	26th Punjab Infantry
3th Battalion	27th Punjabis	27th Punjab Infantry
4th Battalion	28th Punjabis	28th Punjab Infantry
10th Training Battalion	29th Punjabis	29th Punjab Infantry

15th Punjab was mainly recruited from police and tribal levies armed with weapons taken from disbanded mutinous regiments. Enrolled in 1857 to fight the mutineers, they had to wait until 1860 to gain their first honour in China.

All regular battalions participated in the second Afghan War. 2nd and 3rd Battalions fought against the Burmese guerrillas in 1886. The 1st, 2nd and 10th participated in the peacekeeping operations on the North West Frontier. Later, the 2nd went to Egypt and the 3rd took part in the Somalian expedition.

First World War

29th Punjabis was the first Indian unit to sail abroad and to be engaged against the German. They landed in Tsavo (Kenya) in September 1914 to repel an attempted invasion.

Disturbances in China required a sound reinforcement of the Hong-Kong garrison. 1st and 2nd Battalions served there before moving to the Middle East in 1914. The 3rd was posted to the Suez Canal zone and was later part of the Sirhind Brigade of 3rd Lahore Division in France. They went to Iraq and participated in the capture of Baghdad. The 4th garrisoned Ceylon before being sent to Mesopotamia.

In the interwar period, the regiment operated in Waziristan.

Second World War

At the outbreak of the war, the 15th raised ten additional battalions. Most of them remained in India while the 1st, 4th, 6th and 7th fought in Burma. The 2nd was part of 21st Brigade/8th Division and served in Somalia, Syria and Italy.

Partition
The 1st, 2nd, 3rd, 4th and 6th Battalions joined the Pakistan Army.
Last dress uniform
Red, buff facings.
Class composition (1940)
Jats, Pathans, Punjabi Muslims, Sikhs.

Battle Honours
China 1860-62, Ali Masjid, Peiwar Kotal, Charasiah, Ahmed Khel, Kabul 1879, Kandahar 1880, Afghanistan 1878-80, Burma 1885-87, Chitral, Somaliland 1901-04.
Loos, France and Flanders 1915, Suez Canal, Egypt 1915, Megiddo, Sharon, Palestine 1918, Tigris 1916, Kut-al-Amara 1917, Baghdad, Mesopotamia 1915-18, Persia 1918, NW Frontier India 1917, Kilimanjaro, East Africa 1914-17, Berbera, Abyssinia 1940-41, Tug Argan, British Somaliland 1940, West Borneo 1941-42, South East Asia 1941-42, The Sangro, The Moro, Cassino II, Gothic Line, The Senio, Italy 1943-45, Rathedaung, North Arakan, Kohima, Jail Hill, Naga Village, Kyaukmyaung Bridgehead, Mandalay, Fort Dufferin, Meiktila, Nyaungu Bridgehead, Taungtha, The Irrawaddy, Yenaungyaung 1915, Kama, Toungoo, Sittang 1945, Burma 1942-45.

16th Punjab Regiment

BATTALIONS	PREVIOUS TITLE (1903)	19TH CENTURY TITLE
1st Battalion	30th Punjabis	30th Punjab Infantry
2nd Battalion	31th Punjabis	31th Punjab Infantry
3th Battalion	33th Punjabis	33th Punjab Infantry
4th Battalion	9th Bhopal Infantry	The Bhopal Battalion
10th Training Battalion	46th Punjabis	46th Punjab Infantry

1/16th Punjab was raised in 1857 in Ludhiana. Its first name was 22nd Punjab Infantry but in 1861 it was renumbered 30th Bengal Infantry. Along with the 3/16th, the battalion took part in post-Mutiny operations. In 1864, it accompanied the 2/16th to Bhutan and in 1902 it served in China, again with the 2nd. In the meanwhile, it had participated in the second Afghan War and the pacification of the North West Frontier.

First World War

The 4th (Bhopal) was made up of loyal remnants of the Bhopal, Gwalior and Malwa Contingents. In 1914, the Bhopal Infantry raised three more battalions and fought in France with 3rd Lahore Division. The 3/16th went also to France with the Meerut Division. Then, it joined the 1/16th in East of Africa. The other battalions were mainly active in Egypt and in Mesopotamia. After the war, 3rd Battalion participated in the third Afghan War and in the pacification in Iraq.

Second World War

The 2nd and 3rd were captured in Singapore and reconstituted by 5th and 6th Battalions. 4th Battalion was part of 7th Brigade/4th Division which fought in Italy. 1st Battalion served in Burma with 14th Division. 7th Battalion became regular for its distinguished conduct in South East Asia.

Partition
1st, 2nd, 3rd, 4th and 7th Battalions were allotted to the Pakistan Army.
Last dress uniform
Scarlet, white facings, blue lungi and cummerbund.
Class composition (1940)
Dogras, Punjabi Muslims, Sikhs.

Battle Honours
Afghanistan 1878-80, Burma 1885-87, Chitral, Tirah, Punjab Frontier, Malakand.
La Bassée 1914, Messines 1914, Armentieres 1914, Festubert 1914, Givenchy 1914, Ypres 1915, St Julien, Aubers, Loos, France and Flanders 1914-15, Macedonia 1918, Suez Canal, Egypt 1915-16, Megiddo, Nablus, Palestine 1918, Aden, Tigris 1916, Kut-al-Amara 1917, Baghdad, Mesopotamia 1915-18, NW Frontier India 1915, 1916-17, Behobeho, Narungombe, Nyangao, East Africa 1917-18, Afghanistan 1919.
Mescelit Pass, Mt Engiahat, Massawa, Abyssinia 1940-41, Jitra, Ipoh, Kampar, The Muar, Singapore Island, Malaya 1941-42, Sidi Barrani, Omars, Banghazi, El Alamein, Mareth, Akarit, Djebel Garci, Tunis, North Africa 1940-43, Cassino I, Kaladan, Imphal, Tamu Road, Litan, Arakan Beaches, Burma 1942-45.

16th Punjabis, 1919, 1930 and 1944. (Artwork by Mike Chappell)

17th Dogra Regiment

BATTALIONS	PREVIOUS TITLE (1903)	19TH CENTURY TITLE
1st Battalion	37th Dogra	37th Dogra Infantry
2nd Battalion	38th Dogra	38th Dogra Infantry
3th Battalion	1/41st Dogra	41st Dogra Infantry
10th Training Battalion	2/41st Dogra	41st Dogra Infantry

Dogras are Hindus of Rajput origin who settled in the Punjab, Kashmir and Jamı first regiment, recruited exclusively amongst Dogras, was raised in 1887. The second unit was recruited in 1890 and followed by the third in 1900. The 10/17th was a creation of the Great War.

The 37th was immediately involved in the operations of the Black Mountain expedition and the Chitral relief column. The first two battalions were continuously in action on the North West Frontier and in Malakand. 3rd Battalion had the opportunity to go overseas when it sailed to China in 1904.

First World War

1st and 2nd Battalions were engaged in the Middle East and Mesopotamia theatres. The 3rd fought in France, Iraq and Palestine with 7th Meerut Division. In 1930, 1st Battalion was in operation in Burma where it stayed for four years.

Second World War

The twelve battalions of 17th Dogras served in Burma, Malaya or Ceylon. 2nd and 3rd Battalions, captured in Singapore, were reconstituted by 11th and 12th Territorial Battalions.

Partition
The regiment was allotted to the Indian Army (1st, 2nd, 3rd and 4th Battalions).
Last dress uniform
Scarlet, yellow facings.
Class composition (1940)
Dogras.

Battle Honours
Chitral, Malakand, Punjab Frontier, La Bassee 1914, Festubert 1914, 1915, Givenchy 1914, Neuve Chapelle, Aubers, France and Flanders 1914-15, Egypt 1915, Megiddo, Nablus, Palestine 1918, Tigris 1916, Kut-al-Amara 1917, Baghdad, Mesopotamia 1915-18, North-West Frontier, India 1915-17, Afghanistan 1919, Kota Bharu, Malaya 1941-42, Donbaik, Nungshigum, Kennedy Peak, Magwe, Burma 1942-45.

17th Dogras, 1908 and 1930. (Artwork by Mike Chappell)

18th Royal Garhwal Rifles

BATTALIONS	PREVIOUS TITLE (1903)	19TH CENTURY TITLE
1st Battalion	1/39th Garhwal Rifles	1/39th Garhwal Rifles
2nd Battalion	2/39th Garhwal Rifles	2/39th Garhwal Rifles
3th Battalion	3/39th Garhwal Rifles (1914)	
10th Training Battalion	4/39th Garhwal Rifles (1914)	

In January 1891, 39th Regiment of the Bengal Infantry was formed from 2nd Battalion/3rd Gurk
composed entirely of Garhwalis following an order of 1887. In 1892, they were given the title of Rifles. Another regiment
of Garhwalis was raised in 1901 – the 49th – but, shortly afterwards, it became 2nd Battalion of the 39th, making them,
apart from the Gurkhas, the only two-battalion regiment of the Indian Army.

First World War

The 39th was in the Meerut division in the First World War. They were part of 20th Brigade with 2 Leicesters and 2/3
Gurkha Rifles. They suffered heavy casualties in Flanders and were recalled to their base at Lansdown from where they
went to Mesopotamia. Two more battalions were raised during the war and in 1921, they were titled the 39th Royal
Garhwal Rifles.

In 1922, they were the only Indian Infantry regiment to remain intact without being amalgamated. They were
renumbered 18th with the 4th battalion becoming the training battalion (10th).

Second World War

The first three battalions served in different parts, the 2nd being captured by the Japanese in Singapore in 1942. Three
more battalions were raised, one of which, the 5th, was also captured in 1942.

Partition

The Royal Garwhali Rifles were
allocated to India. Having no
Muslims to transfer, it had a
relatively trouble-free handover
(1st, 2nd and 3rd Battalions).

Last dress uniform

Rifle green, red facings.

Class composition (1940)

Garhwalis.

Battle Honours

La Bassée 1914, Armentières 1914, Festubert 1914, Neuve Chapelle, Aubers, Egypt 1915-16,
Khan Baghdadi, Sharquat, Mesopotamia 1917-18, Macedonia 1918, Afghanistan 1919.
Gallabat, Barentu, Keren, Massawa, Amba Alagi, Noth Africa 1940-43, Kuantan, Malaya 1941-
42, Citta di Castello, Italy 1943-45, Yenangyaung 1942, Monywa 1942, Noth Arakan, Ngakyedauk
Pass, Ramree, Taungup, Burma 1942-45.

18th Garhwalis, 1900, 1915 and 1945. (Artwork by Mike Chappell)

19th Hyderabad Regiment
(Kumaon Regiment 1945)

BATTALIONS	PREVIOUS TITLE (1903)	19TH CENTURY TITLE
1st Battalion	94th Russell's Infantry	1er Infantry, Hyderabad Contingent
2nd Battalion	96th Berar Infantry	3rd Infantry, Hyderabad Contingent
3rd Battalion (*)	97th Deccan Infantry	4th Infantry, Hyderabad Contingent
4th Battalion	98th Infantry	5th Infantry, Hyderabad Contingent
5th Battalion (**)	99th Deccan Infantry	6th Infantry, Hyderabad Contingent
10th Training Battalion	95th Russell's Infantry	2nd Infantry, Hyderabad Contingent
(*) disbanded in 1931 (**) disbanded in 1924		

In 1812, Sir Henry Russell, the British resident at Hyderabad, organised the Hyderabad Infantry on the regular system. 1st and 2nd Battalions of the Hyderabad Contingent became 94th and 95th Infantry. Four more battalions were raised in Berar and were joined by two battalions of Salabat Khan, Nawab of Ellichpur, to form the eight battalions of the Hyderabad Infantry. In 1853, the Contingent was reduced to six battalions and participated in the suppression of the 1857 Mutiny.

2nd and 10th Battalions took part in the Burmese campaign of 1885 and 4th Battalion went to China in 1900.

In 1902, the Hyderabad Battalions became units of the new Indian Army.

First World War

The Hyderabad Battalions were present in the Mesopotamia, Egypt and Persia theatres. The 4th went to East Africa.

In 1923, 50th Kumaoni coming from 9th Jat was attached to the regiment.

3rd and 5th Battalions were disbanded in 1931 and 1924, respectively.

Second World War

1st Battalion served in the Middle East, Iran, Burma, French Indochina and Indonesia. In 1946, it was designated to become a parachute battalion. 2nd Battalion fought in Malaya and Burma. 4th Battalion was captured in Singapore. 1/50th Kumaon fought in the Malayan campaign.

Wartime-raised units: eight additional battalions were raised, the 6th and 8th of which went to Burma.

In 1941, the 11/19th gave birth to the 1st Battalion of the Bihar Regiment. In October 1945, the 19th which had lost all links with Hyderabad was re-named The Kumaon Regiment.

Partition
The regiment was allotted to the Indian Army (1st, 2nd, 4th, 6th, 26th Battalions and 1st Kumaon Rifles).
Last dress uniform[1]
Red, green facings.
Class composition (1940)
Jats, Ahirs, Rajput, Kumaoni.

Battle Honours
Nagpore, Meheidpoor, Nowah, Central India, Burma 1885-87, China 1900, Megiddo, Sharon, Palestine 1918, Tigris 1916, Khan Baghdadi, Mesopotamia 1915-18, Persia 1915-18, North West Frontier, India 1914-15, 1916-17, East Africa 1914-16, Afghanistan 1919, North Africa 1940-43, Slim River, Malaya 1941-42, Bishenpur, Kangaw, The Shweli, Magwe, Kama, Sittang 1945, Burma 1942-45.

---

1   Kumaon regiment's uniform: rifle green, black facings.

19th Hyderabad, 1912, 1918 and 1945. (Artwork by Mike Chappell)

20th Burma Rifles

BATTALIONS	PREVIOUS TITLE (1914)
1st Battalion	1/70th Burma Rifles
2nd Battalion	2/70th Burma Rifles
3rd Battalion	85th Burman Rifles (1917)
4th Battalion	4/70th Burma Rifles
10th Training Battalion	5/70th Burma Rifles

Until 1895, the upper Burma region was pacified by the Madras units made up of soldiers from the south west. In 1895, seven battalions were raised in northern India from Sikhs and Punjabi Muslims and nominated as Madras. These battalions would later be renumbered as Punjabis and, subsequently, as Burma Infantry. Karens from Burma were not initially recruited but when they came they were accepted in the Burma Military Police.

In 1916, two companies of Burma pioneers were raised and, by adding two additional companies, it gave birth to 70th Burma Rifles in 1917. In the meantime, 85th Burman Rifles had been formed from the Burma Military Police. The 70th raised a second battalion in 1918 and both units served in the Middle East.

A third battalion was created to suppress the Moplah Rising in Southern India. The 4/70th and 5/70th recruited in 1918, remained in Burma. After the war, the 3/70th was disbanded and it was replaced by the 85th which was renumbered 3/70th.

When 20th Burma Rifles[2] was created in 1923, 1st, 2nd and 3rd Battalions became 1/20th, 2/20th and 3/20th Battalions, respectively while the 5/70th became 10th Training Battalion.

Partition
In 1937, Burma was formally separated from India.
Last dress uniform
Rifle green, red facings.

Class composition (1940)
Karens, Chins, Kachins.

---

2   The 20th Burma Rifles was allotted to the Burmese Army in 1937.

Formations raised during the Second World War

The Bihar Regiment

Created from 1st (Territorial) Battalion, 94th Russell's Infantry. Organised in 1939, it became a four-battalion regiment. Only 1st Battalion saw action in Burma with the Lushai Brigade.

Honours: Haka, Gangaw, Burma 1942-1945.

Partition: allotted to India.

The Assam Regiment

Raised in 1941, it was integrated with the Lushai Scouts in 1942 and was composed of three battalions. 1st Battalion fought in Burma.

Honours: Defence of Kohima, Jessami, Mawlaik, Kyankmyareng, Bridgehead, Tungoo, Aradura, Burma 1942-1945.

Partition: the three battalions went to the India Army.

The Sikh Light Infantry

1st Battalion was raised in 1941 and joined by 2nd, 3rd, 25th and 26th Battalions in 1942. The Sikh LI inherited the traditions of 3rd Sikh Pioneers, born from the amalgamation of 23rd, 33rd and 34th Pioneers. 1st Battalion fought in Burma.

Honours: Taku Forts, Pekin 1860, Abyssinia, Peiwar Kotal, Charasia, Kabul 1879, Kandahar 1880, Afghanistan 1878-1880, Egypt 1915-1917, Gaza, Megiddo, Sharon, Nablus, Palestine 1917-1918, Aden, Defence of Meitkila, Rangoon road, Pyawbwe, Sittang 1945, Burma 1942-1945.

Partition: 1st, 2nd and 3rd Battalions were allotted to the Indian Army.

The Mahar Regiment

Raised in 1941. None of the three battalions saw action. All three were joined to the Indian Army in 1947.

The Badge is inspired by the column of Koregaon which was raised in commemoration of the defence of the town by 2/1st Bombay against the Mahrattas in 1818.

The Ajmer Regiment

Born from 11th (Territorial) Battalion of 4th Bombay Grenadiers. Organised in 1939, it was 26th/4th Grenadiers in 1941 and renamed 1st Battalion Ajmer Regiment in 1942.

2nd Battalion was raised in 1942 and 3rd and 25th Battalions in 1943. The 2nd went to Burma but was reported for misconduct. All battalions were disbanded in 1946.

The Chamar Regiment

Formed from the 27/2nd Punjab. Served in Burma. Disbanded in 1946.

1st Afridi Battalion

After the Khyber Rifles mutiny of 1919, the enlistment of Afridis was stopped.

In 1942, recruitment began for 1st Afridi Battalion to be part of 12th FF Regiment. They quickly moved to Paiforce (Persia and Iraq Force) where they spent most of the war engaged in guard duties. The battalion returned to India for disbandment but was promptly raised again as the Khyber Rifles in the new Pakistani army.

1st Lingayat Battalion

Raised in 1941 at the 10th/5th Mahratta LI Training Centre. The battalion was not considered as an infantry success, was converted to an anti-tank artillery unit and retained by India in 1947.

1st Coorg Battalion

Created from 1st (Territorial) Battalion/83rd Wallajahbad LI. Became 14th Battalion of the 3rd Madras. After the disbandment of 3rd Madras in 1928, it was attached to 1st Madras Pioneers.

When the Madras Pioneers were absorbed into the Engineer Corps, 14th Coorg Battalion had to stand on its own and became a garrison battalion in 1942. In 1946, the battalion was converted to an anti-tank artillery unit and retained by India after Partition.

Wartime raised regiments

The Indian Parachute Regiment

50th Indian Parachute Brigade was created in Delhi in October 1941. Its battle order included:

Brigade HQ,

50 Indian Parachute Brigade Signal Section,

151 British Parachute Battalion,

152 Indian Parachute Battalion,

153 Gurkha Parachute Battalion,

411 (Royal Bombay) Parachute Section, Indian Engineers.

In November 1942, the British battalion moved to Egypt and was replaced by the 3/7th Gurkha, re-named 154th Battalion.

In March 1944, the Brigade was sent to Burma (Impal) to complete its training. Unexpectedly, 152nd and 153rd Battalions found themselves with the 4/5th Mahratta LI facing the Japanese drive north. The five day stand of the Indians earned the XIVth Army a week for a counter-offensive.

The third brigade became 77th Parachute Brigade. In July 1945, the infantry elements of 44 Indian Airborne Division included:

50th Indian Parachute Brigade

16 Para (British),

1 Indian Para Battalion (ex.: 152 battalion),

3 Gurkha Para Battalion (ex.: 154 battalion);

77th Indian Parachute Brigade

15 Para (British),

2 Gurkha Para Battalion (ex.: 153 battalion),

4 Indian Para Battalion (ex: 152 battalion muslim elements);

14th Air Landing Brigade

2 Black Watch,

4/6 Rajputana Rifles,

6/16 Punjab.

In May 1945, a composite Gurkha parachute battalion, formed from 2 and 3 Battalions, landed on Elephant Point at the mouth of the Rangoon River to silence Japanese guns. This was the only action of the regiment in a parachute role.

In November, the division was renumbered as 2nd Indian Airborne Division. All British and Gurkha units were withdrawn from the division, leading to a new organisation.

Division Infantry elements included:

Divisional HQ

1 (Para) Battalion, Kumaon (Defence Battalion) – (I),

3 (Para) Battalion, 15 Punjab (Machine Gun) – (P);

14th Para Brigade

4 (Para) Battalion, Rajputana Rifles – (I),

1 (Para) Battalion, FF Regiment – (P),

3 (Para) Battalion, 16 Punjab – (P);

50th Para Brigade

3 (Para) Battalion, 1 Punjab – (P),

3 (Para) Battalion, Baluch – (P),

2 (Para) Battalion, Madras – (I),

77th Para Brigade

1 (Para) Battalion, 2 Punjab – (I),

3 (Para) Battalion, Mahratta LI – (I),

3 (Para) Battalion, Rajput – (I).

Partition

The eleven parachute battalions were allotted either to India or to Pakistan. Six went to India (I) and five to Pakistan (P).

Last dress uniform

Khaki, maroon beret since 1945.[3]

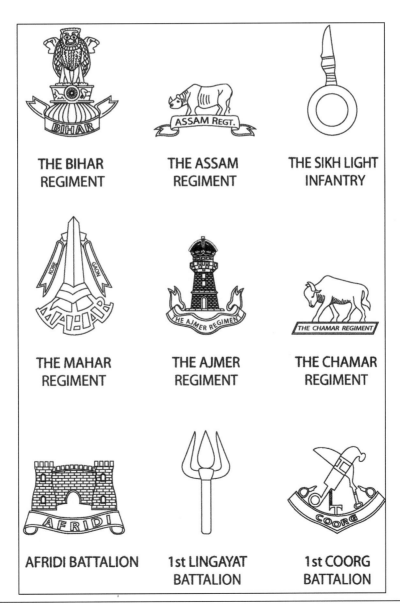

THE BIHAR REGIMENT

THE ASSAM REGIMENT

THE SIKH LIGHT INFANTRY

THE MAHAR REGIMENT

THE AJMER REGIMENT

THE CHAMAR REGIMENT

AFRIDI BATTALION

1st LINGAYAT BATTALION

1st COORG BATTALION

3   Before 1945, battalions wore felt bush hat with cloth battalion badge on the side.

3

The Gurkhas

The Gurkhas occupy a very specific place within the Indian Army. Gurkhas may be described as mercenaries who were enlisted under special treaties between Nepal and India.

After the Treaty of Friendship, which ended the Nepalese Wars of 1814-1816, it was agreed that Gurkha hill men from Nepal should be voluntarily enlisted to serve in the armies of the Honourable East India Company. On the abolition of that Company and transfer of government to the Crown in 1858, the Gurkha Regiments were absorbed into the (British) Indian Army.

In 1816, four battalions of Gurkhas were raised:

1st Nasiri,
2nd Nasiri,
3rd Sirmoor,
4th Kumaon.

In 1826, the 1st Nasiri merged with the 2nd.

During the Mutiny of 1857, the Gurkhas showed exemplary loyalty and participated proudly in all the Indian Army campaigns.

At the end of the First World War, the Gurkhas' strength was ten regiments of two battalions each. The 11th Regiment was raised in 1918 in the Middle East, but its four battalions were disbanded after the war.

During the Second World War, the addition of new Gurkha units increased the strength up to 110,000 soldiers.

On the independence of India, four regiments went into British service while six regiments remained in the Indian Army.

1st King George V's Own Gurkha Rifles
(The Malaun Regiment)

The Gurkha war of 1815-1816 ended when General Ochterlony defeated their army at the Fort of Malaun. The two Nasiri battalions (the word means "friendly") were raised from the defeated Gurkhas at Malaun, hence the title of The Malaun Regiment, conferred in 1903.

1st Nasiri earned its first battle honour at Bhurtpore in 1826 and subsequent honours of Aliwal and Sobraon in the First Sikh War. In 1849, 66th Bengal Native Infantry mutinied at Fort Govindgarh at Amritsar. They were disbanded and ordered to hand over their colours, arms, stores, etc. to 1st Nasiri who assumed the title of the 66th and became a red-coated regiment.

After the Mutiny, they became the 1st Gurkhas. They were the first Gurkha regiment to serve overseas in 1875 when they were sent to Malaya to suppress a rising.

A second battalion was raised in 1886 which took part in the Frontier campaigns of 1897-1898 while 1st Battalion served in Waziristan in 1894. They were little affected by the 1903 changes.

The First World War saw the 1/1st Gurkha Rifles included in the Lahore Division. They fought in France, Flanders, Mesopotamia and Palestine. 2nd Battalion was engaged in small-scale operations on the North West Frontier.

During the Second World War, 1st Battalion took part in the reconquest of Burma after service in Egypt.

In 1945, they went to French Indochina for occupational duties. The 2nd Battalion was posted to Singapore, taken prisoner after the fall of the island and replaced by the 3rd Battalion in 1946.

Partition

In 1947, they became an Indian regiment (1st and 2nd Battalions).

Battle Honours

Bhurtpore, Aliwal, Sobraon, Afghanistan 1878-80, Tirah, Punjab Frontier, Givenchy 1914, Neuve Chapelle, Ypres 1915, St Julien, Festubert 1915, Loos, France and Flanders 1914-15, Megiddo, Sharon, Palestine 1918, Tigris 1916, Kut-al-Amara 1917, Baghdad, Mesopotamia 1916-18, North-West Frontier, India 1915-17, Afghanistan 1919, Jitra, Kampar, Malaya 1941-42, Shenam Pass, Bishenpur, Ukhrul, Myinmu, Bridgehead, Kyaukse 1945, Burma 1942-45.

1st Gurkhas, 1918, 1930 and 1945. (Artwork by Mike Chappell)

2nd King Edward VII's Own Gurkha Rifles
(The Sirmoor Rifles)

2nd Gurkha Rifles sprang from one of the battalions raised from prisoners after the Nepal War. They were called The Sirmoor Battalion because they were originally based in that region. They first attracted attention at the siege of Bhurtpore in 1825 for which they received their first battle honour. In the First Sikh War, the 2nd Gurkha Rifles marched to Ludhiana and fought at Aliwal and Sobraon. The Sirmoors were granted the honour of carrying the "Truncheon"[1] in recognition of their gallant service during the Mutiny.

In 1886, a second battalion was raised. They were with Meerut Division in France during the First World War, after which they served on the Frontier.

The 1st Battalion spent the war in peacekeeping activities in Assam. In 1916, they went to Mesopotamia. During the Second World War, three additional battalions were raised and served in South East Asia. The 1st Battalion fought in Egypt, North Africa and Europe. The 2nd was captured by the Japanese in Singapore and replaced by the 3rd Battalion in 1946. The wartime battalions (3rd, 4th, and 5th) served in South East Asia.

Partition

The 2nd Gurkhas was one of the regiments which joined the British Army (1st and 2nd Battalions).

Battle Honours

Bhurtpore, Aliwal, Sobraon, Delhi 1857, Kabul 1879, Kandahar 1880, Afghanistan 1878-80, Tirah, Punjab Frontier, La Bassee 1914, Festubert 1914-15, Givenchy 1914, Neuve Chapelle, Aubers, Loos, France and Flanders 1914- 15, Egypt 1915, Tigris 1916, Kut-al-Amara 1917, Baghdad, Mesopotamis 1916-18, Persia 1918, Baluchistan, 1918, Afghanistan 1919, El Alamein, Mareth, Akarit, Djebel el Meida, Enfidaville, Tunis, North Africa 1942-43, Cassino I, Monastery Hill, Pian di Maggio, Gothic Line, Coriano, Poggio San Giovanni, Monte Reggiano, Italy 1944-45, Greece 1944¬45, North Malaya, Jitra, Central Malaya, Kampar, Slim River, Johore, Singapore Island, Malaya 1941-42, North Arakan, Irrawaddy, Magwe, Sittang 1945, Point 1433, Arakan Beaches, Myebon, Tamandu, Chindits 1943, Burma 1942-45.

---

1   Bronze staff, 6ft. high, surmounted by three figures of Gurkha soldiers of the Mutiny period supporting a silver crown.

2nd Gurkhas, 1857, 1830 and 1943. (Artwork by Mike Chappell)

3rd Queen Alexandra's Own Gurkha Rifles

1st Battalion was raised in 1816 to police the Nepalese border. In 1857, they marched to Delhi and assaulted the Kashmir Gate. In 1865, they went on campaign to Bhutan. Their next action was during the second Afghan War when they marched to Kandahar and were assaulted in Ahmed Khel. The 3rd Gurkha Rifles participated also in the third Burma War.

A second battalion was raised in 1887 and became the 39th Garhwalis in 1891. Both battalions were engaged in the Tirah campaign of 1897 and in Waziristan in 1901.

During the First World War, the 2nd battalion saw action in France and Palestine. During the Second World War, the 1st battalion fought in Burma and the 2nd campaigned in Egypt, Palestine and Italy where they were part of the 20th Brigade of the 10th Division. The 3rd Battalion was raised in 1940 and served in Asia.

Partition

3rd Gurkha Rifles remained in the Indian Army (1st, 2nd and 3rd Battalions).

Battle Honours

Delhi 1857, Ahmed Khel, Afghanistan 1878-80, Burma 1885-87, Chitral, Tirah, Punjab Frontier, La Bassee 1914, Armentieres 1914, Festubert 1914-15, Givenchy 1914, Neuve Chapelle, Aubers, France and Flanders 1914-15, Egypt1915-16, Gaza, El Mughar, Nebi Samwil, Jerusalem, Tell-Asur, Megiddo, Sharon, Palestine 1917-18, Sharqat, Mesopotamia 1917-18, Afghanistan 1919, Deir el Shein, North Africa 1940-43, Monte Della Gorgace, II Castello, Monte Farneto, Monte Cavallo, Italy 194-3-45, Sittang 1942, Kyaukse 1942, Imphal, Tuitum, Sakawng, Shenam Pass, Bishenpur, Tengnoupal, Meiktila, Defence Of Meiktila, Rangoon Road, Pyawbwe, Pegu 1945, Burma 1942-45.

3rd Gurkhas, 1918, 1930 and 1945. (Artwork by Mike Chappell)

4th Prince of Wales' Own Gurkha Rifles

4th Gurkhas was raised in 1857 and, in 1868, it was part of the force which was ordered to suppress a group of Pathan fanatics. 4th Gurkha Rifles took part in the second Afghan War.

In 1886, a second battalion was created and immediately sent to the North West Frontier. In 1900, the 1/4th sailed to China to suppress the Boxer Rebellion.

In 1914, the 1st Battalion fought in France and Gallipoli. The 2nd went to Mesopotamia and they were among the first to enter Baghdad.

During the Second World War, the 1/4th served in India and Burma. The 2/4th fought in Egypt and Italy with 10th Division. A third and fourth battalion were raised in 1940 and 1941 respectively to serve in Burma, the 3/4th being part of the famous 77th Brigade of Wingate.

Partition

The regiment remained a unit of the Indian Army (1st, 2nd and 3rd Battalions)

Battle Honours

Ali Masjid, Kabul 1879, Kandahar 1880, Afghanistan 1878-80,Waziristan 1895, Chitral, Tirah, Punjab Frontier, China 1900, Givenchy 1914, Neuve Chapelle,Ypres 1915, St Julien, Aubers, Festubert 1915, France and Flanders 1914-15, Gallipoli 1915, Egypt 1916, Tigris 1916, Kut-al¬Amara 1917, Baghdad, Mesopotamia 1916-18, North-West Frontier, India 1917, Baluchistan 1918, Afghanistan 1919, Iraq 1941, Syria 1941, The Cauldron, North Africa 1940-43, Trestina, Monte Cedrone, Italy 194-3-45, Pegu 1942, Chindits 1944, Mandalay, Burma 1942-45.

4th Gurkhas, 1908, 1930 and 1945. (Artwork by Mike Chappell)

5th Royal Gurkha Rifles
(Frontier Force)

5th Gurkha Rifles was raised in 1858 as the Hazara Gurkha battalion. Their first fight was against the Mahsuds in 1860. The regiment achieved its reputation during the second Afghan War when they fought the rearguard action at the Mangiar defile and in the battle of Charasia.

The second battalion was recruited in 1886 and its first significant action came during the Black Mountain expedition of 1891.

During the Great War, the 1/5th suffered heavily at Gallipoli. The last allied troops to leave the Peninsula were C. Company of 1/5th Gurkhas. The second battalion served in Mesopotamia and a third battalion, raised in 1916, fought in Iraq.

In 1919, the regiment served in the third Afghan War. Until 1939, they operated on the North West Frontier. In 1921, the 5th Gurkha Rifles was given the title of "Royal" and permitted to wear a red lanyard.[2] During the Second World War, the 1st Battalion served in Iran, Iraq, Egypt and Italy. 2nd Battalion served in Burma and Japan.

A third battalion was raised in October 1940 and campaigned in Burma, Malaya and the Dutch East Indies. A fourth battalion was raised in March 1941 to serve in Burma and was disbanded in December 1946.

Partition

The 1st, 2nd and 3rd Battalions went to the Indian Army.

Battle Honours

Peiwar Kotal, Charasiah, Kabul. 1879, Kandshar 1880, Afghanistan 1878-80, Punjab Frontier, Helles, Krithia, Suvla, Sari Bair, Gallipoli 1915, Suez Canal, Egypt 1915-16, Khan Baghdadi, Mesopotamia 1916-18, North-West Frontier, India 1917, Afghanistan 1919, North West Frontier 1930, North West Frontier 1936-39, The Sangro, Caldari, Cassino II, Sant'Angelo inTeodice, Rocca d'Arce, Rippa Ridge, Femmina Morte, Monte San Bartolo, Italy 1943-45, Sittang 1942, 1945, Kyaukse 1942,Yenangyaung 1942, Stockades, Buthidaung, Imphal, Sakawng, Bishenpur, Shenam Pass, The Irrawaddy, Burma 1942-45.

---

2   The other regiments wear a green and black one.

5th Gurkhas, 1895, 1918 and 1946. (Artwork by Mike Chappell)

6th Gurkha Rifles

They were the first of the Gurkha regiments to start life as a unit recruited from plainsmen. They were raised in Orissa in 1817 and were initially called The Cuttock Legion. In 1823, they moved to Northern Bengal as the Rangpur Light Infantry. It was at that stage that the first Gurkhas were enlisted. In 1886, they became a class regiment of Gurkhas only, having fought until then on the Assam border and in Burma. The second battalion was raised in 1904.

During the First World War, 1st Battalion fired their first shots at Kantara in January 1915 when the Turks attempted to seize the Suez Canal. They were shipped to Gallipoli later that year and were the first Gurkhas to land there. The 6th Gurkha Rifles are best known for their bravery in that ill-fated battle. After the retreat, the 1/6th met the 2/6th, coming from Mesopotamia and Salonika, on the Caspian Sea.

A temporary 3rd Battalion (1917-1921) fought in Waziristan and Afghanistan.

During the Second World War, the 1/6th saw action in Burma and the 2/6th in Italy. The reborn 3rd Battalion was part of the famous 3rd (Chindit) Division.

Partition

The 6th Gurkha Rifles went to the Gurkha Brigade of the British Army (1st and 2nd Battalions).

Battle Honours

Burma 1885-87, Helles, Krithia, Suvla, Sari Bair, Gallipoli 1915, Suez Canal, Egypt 1915-16, Khan Baghdadi, Mesopotamia 1916-18, Persia 1918, North West Frontier, India 1915, Afghanistan 1919, Coriano, Santarcangelo, Monte Chicco, Lamone Crossing, Senio Floodbank, Medicina, Gaiana Crossing, Italy 1944-45, Shwebo, Kyaukmyaung Bridgehead, Mandalay, Fort Dufferin, Mayrnyo, Rangoon Road, Toungoo, Sittang 1945, Chindits 1944, Burma 1942.

6th Gurkhas, 1910 and 1930. (Artwork by Mike Chappell)

7th Gurkha Rifles
(Duke of Edinburgh's Own)

7th Gurkhas were formed at Quetta in North West India, recruited from clans of Eastern Nepal. In 1908, a second battalion was raised.

The 2/7th's baptism of fire was in 1915 defending the Suez Canal against the Turks, and their first major battle honour was won at Naseriya, advancing through Mesopotamia the same year. The campaign turned into a disaster and while 2/7th made an epic stand at Ctesiphon, the battalion was captured by the Turks following the fall of Kut in April 1916. The reformed 2/7th was in action in the Middle East at Ramadi in 1916 and in Palestine in 1918 where 1/7th also won a battle honour at Sharquat.

In the interwar period, the 7th soldiered on in Afghanistan and on the North West Frontier. In May 1941, 2/7th was committed to action in Iraq and the occupation of Iran and, as part of 4th Indian Division, they fought doggedly in the defence of Tobruk. At the end of the siege in June 1941, 2/7th went into captivity.

A new 2/7th was raised and fought in the long slog up Italy – at Cassino, Monte Grillo and the attack on the Gothic Line. Before returning to India in December 1945, they were briefly in action during the Greek civil war.

1/7th and 3/7th (raised in 1940) were, meanwhile, on the Burma/Thai border when the Japanese struck at the end of 1941. Fighting rearguard actions all the way to the Indian frontier, they were decimated in the crossing of the Sittang River. The survivors joined together to form one unit and, with 17th Indian Division, they held the road to Imphal through 1943, offering determined resistance during the last Japanese offensive of March/June 1944. 1/7th were at the fore of the fighting during the reconquest of Burma in January 1945. In December 1942, the 3/7th Gurkha Rifles were converted to a parachute battalion.

Partition

7th Gurkha Rifles joined the British army (1st and 2nd Battalions).

Battle Honours

Suez Canal, Egypt 1915, Megiddo, Sharon, Palestine 1918, Shaiba, Kut-al-Amara 1915,1917, Ctesiphon, Baghdad, Sharqat, Mesopotamia 1915-18, Afghanistan 1919, Tobruk 1942, North Africa 1942, Cassino I, Campriano, Poggio del Grillo, Tavoleto, Montebello-Scorticata Ridge, Italy 1944, Pegu 1942, Kyaukse 1942, Shwegyin, Imphal, Bishenpur, Meiktila, Capture of Meiktila, Defence of Meiktila, Rangoon Road, Pyawbwe, Burma 1942-45.

7th Gurkhas, 1944 and 1945. (Artwork by Mike Chappell)

8th Gurkha Rifles

The two regiments forming 8th Gurkha Rifles were created on the North East Frontier. The 16th Sylhet Local Battalion was raised in February 1824 and the Lower Assam Sebundy Corps was created in 1839. They assumed a Gurkha title only in 1886 and were mainly engaged in operations on the Burmese border and against the Nagas tribes of Assam. In 1903, the 1/8th took part in the Tibet expedition. The two units were merged in 1907 to form 1st and 2nd Battalions of the 8th Gurkha Rifles.

During the Great War, the 1st Battalion was engaged in Mesopotamia and Egypt. The 2nd Battalion fought in France in 21st Bareilly Brigade. In 1921, the 2/8th was in action on the south-western coast of India to suppress the Moplah rebellion.

During the Second World War, the 1/8th fought in Burma and Indonesia. The 2/8th campaigned in Iraq and Egypt before being sent to Italy with 43rd Independent Brigade 12. A third battalion, raised in 1940 and disbanded in 1947, and a fourth battalion, raised in 1941, fought in the Far East.

Partition

The 8th Gurkha Rifles remained in the Indian Army (1st, 2nd and 4th Battalions).

Battle Honours

Burma 1885-87, La Bassee 1914, Festubert 1914, 1915, Givenchy 1914, Neuve Chapelle, Aubers, France and Flanders 1914-15, Egypt 1915-16, Megiddo, Sharon, Palestine 1918, Tigris 1916, Kut-al-Amara 1917, Baghdad, Mesopotamia 1916-17, Afghanistan 1919, Iraq 1941, North Africa 1940¬43, Gothic Line, Coriano, Santarcangelo, Gaiana Crossing, Point 551, Imphal, Tamu Road, Bishenpur, Kanglatongbi, Mandalay, Myinmu Bridgehead, Singhu, Shandatgyi, Sittang 1945, Burma 1942-45.

8th Gurkhas, 1929, 1930 and 1945. (Artwork by Mike Chappell)

9th Gurkha Rifles

The beginnings of 9th Gurkhas can be traced to the year 1817 when the Fatehgarh Levy was created. The regiment fought in Sobraon, during the second Afghan War and during the Tirah campaign (1897-1898). In 1901, they were renamed 9th Gurkha Rifles.

Incorporated into 7th Meerut Division, the 1/9th took part in battles in France before being sent to Mesopotamia where it met its brother, 2nd Battalion. The 2/9th Gurkha Rifles were also involved in the suppression of the Moplah rebellion of 1921.

During the Second World War, the battalions were employed in different theatres of operations:

The 1/9 was integrated into 5th Brigade/4th Division and travelled intensively in Iraq, Iran, Egypt, North Africa, Italy and Greece;

The 2/9th was captured by the Japanese in Singapore;

The 3/9th and 4/9th were raised in 1940 and fought in Burma with 3rd (Chindit) Division.

Partition

9th Gurkha Rifles were one of the six regiments which remained part of the Indian Army (1st, 2nd and 3rd Battalions).

Battle Honours

Bhurtpore, Sobraon, Afghanistan 1879-80, Punjab Frontier, La Bassee 1914, Armentieres 1914, Festubert 1914, 1915, Givenchy 1914, Neuve Chapelle, Aubers, Loos , France and Flanders 191415, Tigris 1916, Kut-al-Amara 1917, Baghdad, Mesopotamia 1916-18, Afghanistan 1919, Djebel el Meida, Djebel Garci, Ragoubet Souissi, North Africa 1940-43, Cassino I, Hangman's Hill, Tavoleto, San Marino, Italy 1943-45, Greece 1944-45, Malaya 1941-42, Chindits 1944, Burma 1942-45.

9th Gurkhas, 1897, 1918 and 1930. (Artwork by Mike Chappell)

10th Gurkha Rifles
(Princess Mary's Own)

10th Gurkha Rifles started out as a police unit created in 1887 to keep order in Burma. In 1903, 10th Madras Infantry became 10th Gurkha Rifles and a second battalion was raised in 1908.

1/10th Gurkha Rifles spent the early part of the First World War fighting tribes on the northern border of Burma. They were then sent to Mesopotamia to provide protection for the railway construction and, finally, they participated in the offensive on Baghdad. They stayed in Mesopotamia for four years after the end of the war.

2nd Gurkha Rifles went to Gallipoli with two other Gurkha Battalions (1/5th and 1/6th) where it lost 75% of its officers and 40% of other ranks. In the Second World War, 1st, 3rd and 4th Battalions were engaged in the Burmese campaign. 2nd Battalion fought in Syria and Italy. During the war, 10th Gurkhas won more gallantry awards than any other regiment in the Indian Army.

Partition
In 1947, the 10th was allotted to the British Army (1st and 2nd battalions).

Battle Honours
Suez Canal, Egypt 1915, Megiddo, Sharon, Palestine 1918, Shaiba, Kut-al-Amara 1915, 1917, Ctesiphon, Defence of Kut-al-Amara, Baghdad, Sharqat, Mesopotamia 1915-18, Afghanistan 1919, Tobruk 1942, North Africa 1942, Cassino I, Campriano, Poggio del Grillo, Tavoleto, Montbello-Scorticata Ridge, Italy 1944, Sittang 1942, 1945, Pegu 1942, Kyaukse 1942, Shwegyin, Imphal, Bishenpur, Meiktila, Capture of Meiktila, Defence of Meiktila, Rangoon Road, Pyawbwe, Burma 1942-45.

10th Gurkhas, 1911, 1920 and 1946. (Artwork by Mike Chappell)

Other Units and Corps

6.1 Mountain Artillery

After the Indian Mutiny, the British government was more than ever unwilling to give the Indian Army access to heavy weapons. That is the reason why there were only 12 Mountain Batteries of six guns each in the 1914 table of organisation. The guns were carried on mules. All artillery officers were British from the Royal Artillery.

The batteries numbered from one to 20 were part of the British troops in India while most of the subordinates were native Indians. The Indian batteries were numbered from 21 to 32.

Indian Mountain Artillery

21st Royal (Kohat) Mountain Battery (FF)	1851
22nd (Dejarat) Mountain Battery (FF)	1849
23rd (Peshawar) Mountain Battery (FF)	1853
24th (Hazara) Mountain Battery (FF)	1851
25th (Bombay) Mountain Battery	1827
26th (Jacob's) Mountain Battery	1843
27th (Bengal) Mountain Battery	1886
28th (Lahore) Mountain Battery	1886
29th (Murree) Mountain Battery	1898
30th (Abbottabad) Mountain Battery	1900
31st (Dehra Dun) Mountain Battery	1907
32nd (Poonch) Mountain Battery	1907

During the First World War, 15 additional batteries were raised, six of which were disbanded in 1921.

In 1935, the first Indian Field Artillery Regiment was formed; it consisted of four horse-drawn batteries. In 1939, the artillery became a separate arm of service. During the Second World War, the Indian artillery expanded to 64 regiments of field, anti-tank and mainly anti-aircraft artillery.

6.2 The Engineer Corps

The Corps of Sappers and Miners was in charge of conventional military engineering duties:

> building and fortification,
> obstacle and river crossing,
> road opening and maintenance,
> mining and sapping,
> military railroad.

Until 1920, the Corps also controlled the Signal Companies.

In 1914, the Corps was composed of:

> 1st King George's Own Sappers & Miners (ex-Bengal) – companies 1 to 6 – based in Gurki;
> 2nd Queen Victoria's Own Sappers & Miners (ex-Madras) – companies 9 to 15 – based in Jask;
> 3rd Sappers & Miners (ex-Bombay) – companies 17 to 22 – based in Kirkee;

Artillery, 1910 and 1939. (Artwork by Mike Chappell)

and independent companies:

25th and 26th Railway,
31st to 34th Divisional Signal,
41st Wireless Signal.

In 1920, the Signal Companies were transferred to the Signal Corps.
In 1923, the three regiments formed the Indian Engineer Corps.

6.3 Pioneers

There were two generations of Pioneers in the Indian Army. The first generation dates back to the 18th century: it evolved into Sappers and Miners with more and more specialised engineering tasks. The second generation began service as infantry of the line, preparing the road for the main corps of infantry. This included road and railway building, irrigation projects, dam construction and barrack-building.

From 1864 to 1904, the number of pioneer infantry battalions grew from two to twelve.

At the outbreak of the First World War, every infantry division had one pioneer battalion trained as infantry but also carrying light engineering equipment.

In the post-war reform, the Pioneers were taken out of the infantry of the line and grouped into four Pioneer regiments, taking precedence over the infantry (1st Madras Pioneers, 2nd Bombay Pioneers, 3rd Sikh Pioneers and 4th Hazara Pioneers). In just ten years, their tasks became so specific and their efficiency as infantry so compromised that they had actually become engineers, duplicating the work of the Sappers and Miners. The Pioneers were therefore disbanded in 1933 and absorbed into the Engineers Corps.

6.4 Services

6.4.1 The Supply and Transport Corps (STC)

Before the Great War, India had no military mechanical transport. The supply and distribution of food, forage and ammunitions to the units were tasks performed by horses and mules. The first motorised transportation driven by British territorials appeared at the end of the war.

After 1918, STC became the Indian Army Service Corps. The title "Royal" was granted in 1935. A RIASC unit was the first Indian outfit to land in France in 1939.

6.4.2 The Military Farms Department

Until 1912, this organisation was part of the STC. Their role was the maintenance of grass and dairy farms. During the Second World War, their role was expanded to meat supply.

6.4.3 The Medical Corps

The military health services of the Indian Army were divided into four departments:

The Indian Medical Service was composed only of officer personnel and constituted a reserve of superior medical staff.

The Indian Medical Department was formed by medical staff in charge of the British Army in India (assistant surgeons) and of the Indian troops (sub-assistant surgeons).

The Indian Military Nursing Service was created during the Great War to train and provide skilled nursing orderlies.

The Indian Hospital Corps was a result of an amalgamation of the Army Hospital Corps with the Indian Bearer Corps. This corps had the mission to provide treatment to the sick and wounded and to train stretcher-bearers. During the Second World War, all these services and corps were merged into the Indian Army Medical Corps.

6.4.4 The Remount and Veterinary Service

Given the large number of animals used by the Indian Army, the Remount and Veterinary Service survived until 1947.

Cavalry units had their own veterinary officer called "salutri".

6.4.5 The Ordnance Department

The Corps started as an offshoot of the Artillery. It became the Indian Army Ordnance Corps in 1929.

Sappers and Miners, 1918, 1930 and 1945. (Artwork by Mike Chappell)

Medical Service, 1916 and 1918. (Artwork by Mike Chappell)

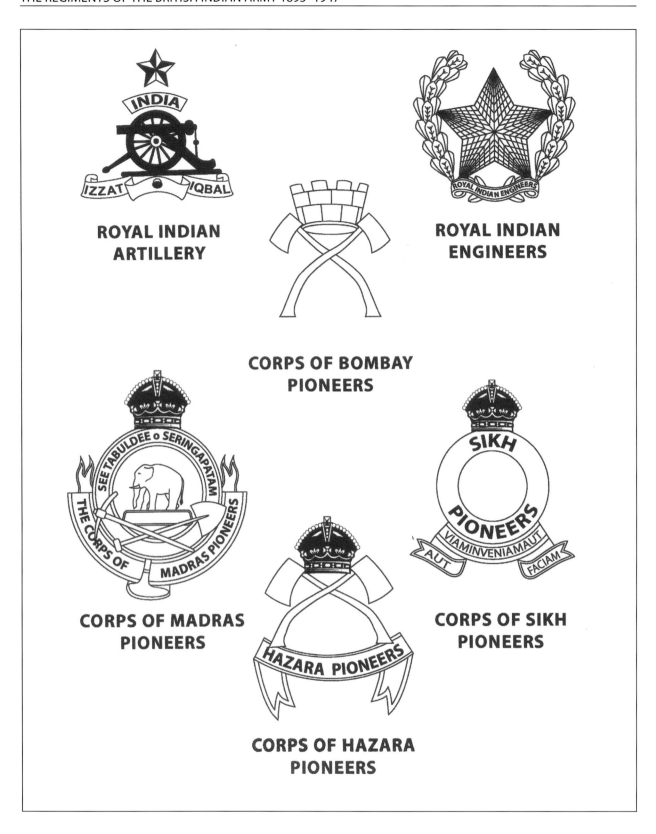

ROYAL INDIAN ARTILLERY

CORPS OF BOMBAY PIONEERS

ROYAL INDIAN ENGINEERS

CORPS OF MADRAS PIONEERS

CORPS OF HAZARA PIONEERS

CORPS OF SIKH PIONEERS

In 1943, some of its members, along with Engineers, formed the Corps of Indian Electrical and Mechanical Engineers.

6.4.6 The Indian Signal Corps
Created in 1920 by integrating the Signal Companies of the Sappers and Miners.

6.4.7 The Indian Corps of Clerks
Created in 1924 to fulfil administration tasks. It became the Indian Army Corps of Clerks in 1942.

ROYAL INDIAN ARMY SERVICE CORPS

INDIAN SIGNAL CORPS

INDIAN ARMY ORDNANCE CORPS

INDIAN ARMY REMOUNT VETERINARY SERVICES

INDIAN MEDICAL SERVICE

MILITARY FARM DEPARTMENT

6.4.8 The Corps of Military Police India

Formed in 1942 to enforce discipline and guard prisoner of war camps. Before the war, these tasks were duties of the regimental police.

6.5 Princely State Armies

Almost a quarter of the population of the subcontinent lived not under the rule of the British, but in over a hundred semi-independent princely states which had entered into treaty relationships, first with the East India Company and later with the Crown. These states maintained their own armed forces, usually supplied with British officers. In some cases,

Mysore Lancers, 1910 and 1919. (Artwork by Mike Chappell)

Jodhpur Lancers, 1910 and 1919

Gwalior, Patiala and Bikaner officers, 1900. (Artwork by Bruno Mugnai)

the states' rulers formed EIC troops for their own protection. In the case of the large state of Hyderabad, the Crown maintained a small army known as the Hyderabad Contingent as well as the state's own small forces. Technological progress eventually rendered most of the state forces useless for anything but ceremonial duties.

In 1885, about a score of the states participated in the Imperial Service Troops (IST) scheme to train up some of their forces to standard and make them available for emergencies.

During the First World War, 18,000 soldiers from these troops served overseas. Some had an opportunity to distinguish themselves, as in the case of the Jodhpur Lancers from 15th Cavalry Brigade who seized Haïfa during the Palestine offensive. After the war, these were reorganised into several classes of readiness of Indian States Forces (ISF).

During the Second World War, 49 states fielded 50,000 men ranging from platoon to division strength. The 34th Infantry Brigade was entirely made up of IST troops. In 1945, the 150th Hong Kong Brigade was composed of three State Force Battalions. Other units of the IST served also actively in Italy, Greece and Burma.

During post-war negotiations for independence, it became clear that India would not tolerate the existence of these princely states. Most of the rulers accepted integration into India.

6.6 The Auxiliary Force India (AFI)

After the Mutiny, many self-defence units were constituted by Europeans. Most of them remained purely European, others recruited also from Anglo-Indians and natives. In 1907, the Indian Volunteer Force had a strength of 34,000 men.

In 1917, all Europeans between 18 and 41 years of age were integrated into the Indian Defence Force.

After the war, many units were disbanded and the Auxiliary Force India continued to perform local service and guard duties.

During the Second World War, the Auxiliary Force regained its role as the reserve pool of officers while protecting the communications. Men from both units of the AFI, the Calcutta Light Horse and the Calcutta Scottish, boarded a German spy ship in the port of Goa.

In 1947, the Auxiliary Force had no reason to exist anymore and was disbanded.

6.7 The Frontier Corps[1]

The security of the Frontier was a permanent concern for the Commander-in-Chief. A new Frontier policy was launched: the army was to be withdrawn from tribal territory and replaced with disciplined tribal irregulars led by their leaders and seconded by British officers.

Thus, the following troops were formed on the North West Frontier:

The Khyber Rifles,
The Waziristan militia,
The Kurram militia,
The Zhob militia,
The Chitral Scouts,
The Gilgit Scouts;
and on the North East Frontier: the Assam Rifles.

In 1914, the entire Frontier was covered. However, the Third Afghan War of 1919 led to desertions and other issues among the Khyber Rifles and the Waziristan militia. Both units were undermined by the preaching of the Muslim mullahs and offered discharge. Later, the militias of Waziristan were reconstituted and renamed Tochi Scouts and Waziristan Scouts.

The Frontier Corps remained active until 1947 bearing the brunt of the tribesmen's hostile activities. At partition, all units of the North West went to Pakistan. The Assam Rifles joined the Indian Army.

---

1 Not to be confused with the Frontier Force of the Indian Army.

Epilogue

In his book, *A Matter of Honour*, Philip Mason wrote that the value of an army lies rather in human factors than merely in its equipment. If there were to be one example that supports this statement, the history of the Indian Army would be the perfect one.

Little affected by the issues faced by the civil society in the 20th century, the Indian Army remained loyal to its word, to *izzat*. In so doing, the army cultivated a spirit that enabled it to carry on through the subcontinent's history of upheaval without flinching.

Labelled by some as an "army of mercenaries", the Indian Army continually gave the lie to this label. Nowhere does history record that Indian soldiers switched sides in order to obtain material advantage. Of course, mutinies, revolts and desertions were recorded, but these were always due to either the rigid observance of caste or religious norms, or – in most cases – the tactlessness, ignorance, or disdain of European officers.[1]

It cannot be denied that, during the Indian Mutiny, men from the north – Sikhs, Pathans, Punjabis and Baluchis – were driven as much by plunder promises as they were by the need to put down the Bengali revolt. However, from 1858 onwards, it was these same soldiers who endured the ambushes in the Burmese forests, the cold of the Tibetan mountain ranges and the fighting in the shadow of the far-off Wall of China.

What about the perilous fighting in Afghanistan and on the North West Frontier, where they often fought to the last man in defence of the honour of their regiment?

And what about the 34,000 dead and 70,000 wounded during the Second World War?

Fortunately, the large number of Victoria Crosses and other battle honours is there to bear witness to the valour and sacrifice of an army which found itself involved in conflicts that were not even its own. Nevertheless, the Indian Army, ill equipped and poorly trained to fight overseas, proved itself to be the equal of the best armies in the world. And when the time came to close that chapter of history, the Indian Army bequeathed the essential tools to the new independent states to ensure their legitimacy at the time they needed it most.

---

1   The destiny of the Indian National Army (INA) cannot be considered in the scales of history alongside the unflagging loyalty of the Indian Army during the critical period leading up to Independence.

Appendix I

Ranks in the Indian Army

British Army	Indian Cavalry	Indian Infantry
Captain	*Risaldar-major*	*Subedar-major*
Lieutenant	*Risaldar*	*Subedar*
2nd lieutenant	*Jemadar*	*Jemadar*
Sergeant-major	*Kat-Dafadar*	*Havildar-major*
Sergeant	*Dafadar*	*Havildar*
Corporal	*Lance-Dafadar*	*Naik*
Lance-Corporal	Acting *Lance-Dafadar*	*Lance-Naik*
Private	*Sowar*	*Sepoy*

The Subedar- (*Risaldar*) major was the highest ranking native officer in the unit. He was qualified to give advice to the commanding officer on Indian matters.

There were three categories of Indian officer:

VCO – Viceroy's Commissioned Officer, ex NCO stepping from the ranks;

KCIO – King's Commissioned Indian Officer, graduated from the Sandhurst Military Academy;

ICO – Indian Commissioned Officer, graduated from the Dehra Dun Military Academy.

The Indianisation of the Indian Army was accelerated during the Second World War through the creation of Indian Emergency Commissioned Officers (IECO).

Appendix II

Some personalities of Indian Military History

Claude AUCHINLECK (1884-1981)

Born in Ulster in 1884.

Educated at Sandhurst.

Commissioned to the 62nd Punjab Regiment where he saw action in Egypt, Aden and Mesopotamia.

Was given control of the Meerut District in 1938.

On 7 May 1940, he was sent to command 25,000 British, French and Polish troops in Norway.

Returned to India in 1941.

Commander-in-Chief of British troops in the Middle East against the Afrika Korps of Rommel.

Replaced by Alexander in August 1942.

On 20 June 1943, replaced Wavell as Commander-in-Chief of the British Army in India.

Field Marshal in June 1945.

Was given the task of splitting the Indian Army. Accused of being partial to the Pakistanis, he resigned in August 1947.

Died in 1981 after having held several administrative posts.

Samuel BROWNE (1824-1901)

Born in Bengal. Son of a surgeon.

At the age of 16, joined the 46th Regiment of Bengal Native Infantry as ensign.

Fought the second Sikh War and served on the North West Frontier.

Took command of the 2nd Punjab Cavalry.

Won a Victoria Cross and lost his arm when attacking a rebel field gun at Seerporah.

Designed the famous Sam Browne belt to cope with his disability.

Commanded the Peshawar Field Force during the second Afghan War and captured Ali Masjid.

Died in 1901 on the Isle of Wight.

Robert CLIVE (1725-1774)

In 1743, he accepted the low position of writer in the East India Company.

When the French captured Madras, he escaped and accepted a position in the army as an ensign.

In 1751, then captain, captured Arcot compelling the French to give up the siege of Trichinopoly.

Clive's victories broke French power in India and gave the British a stronghold.

Returned to India again as Governor of Fort St-David, recaptured Calcutta and defeated the Nawab at Plassey, permanently embedding British power in India.

Was elevated to the peerage and became Governor and Commander-in-Chief in Bengal.

Ill health forced him to return to England in 1767.

Disgrace, continued illness and addiction to opium resulted in his suicide in 1774.

Joseph DUPLEIX (1697-1763)

Son of a leading member of the French East India Company.

Governor of Pondicherry and Governor General of all French establishments in India.

Started the war against the British in 1742.

Captured Madras and forced the Company to lift the siege of Pondicherry.

Supported the Indian sovereigns against England.

Disgraced for his first failures, went back to France in 1754 and died in poverty.

HAIDAR ALI (1722-1782) also Hayder Ali

A Muslim of peasant stock, he rose by military brilliance to command the army of Mysore.

By 1761, was virtual ruler of Mysore and began expanding the kingdom at the expense of the Mahratta States and Hyderabad.

In 1764, the British took the field against him. This first war ended without clear results.

In 1780, Haidar invaded the Carnatic and routed a British Force.

Was defeated near Madras in 1781 and died a year later.

The war was continued by his son Tipu Sultan.

Warren HASTINGS (1732-1818)

Employed as a clerk by the East India Company.

Rose quickly through the ranks.

Disgusted with corruption, returned to England in 1764.

Went back to India in 1769 and became Governor of Bengal in 1772.

First Governor General of India in 1774. Despatched armies from Bengal that saved the British position.

Resigned and returned to England in 1784.

Charged with high crimes but exculpated at trial. Became a private counsellor.

William HODSON (1821-1858)

Third son of Rev. Georges Hodson.

Educated at Rugby and Cambridge.

Joined the 2nd Bengal Grenadiers, went to the first Sikh War and was present at the battles of Moodkee, Ferozeshah and Sobraon.

Was empowered to raise a regiment of irregular horse in 1857 and placed at the head of the Intelligence department.

Played a large part in the reduction of Delhi and consequently in saving India for the British Empire.

Captured Bahadur Shah and his sons. Obtained the unconditional surrender of the three princes. In front of a large and threatening crowd, he shot them dead with his own hand.

Hodson was killed on 11 March 1858 in the attack on Lucknow.

It was said of him that he never received the Victoria Cross because he would have earn it every day of his life.

MALHAR RAO HOLKAR (1694-1766)

Rose from peasant origins by his own ability.

Received command of a body of 500 horsemen due to his soldierly prowess.

In 1733, Peshwa gifted him the Indore area.

Became gradually independent and owned a vast territory stretching from the Deccan to the Malwa.

Founder of the dynasty "Holkar of Indore".

JASWANT RAO HOLKAR

After the defeat of the Scindias of Gwalior in 1803, he took on the British Forces and defeated Colonel W. Monson. He besieged Delhi.

Defeated by Lord Lake in 1804, was compelled to make peace.

Became insane and died in 1811.

Horatio KITCHENER (1850-1916)

Educated at the RMA. Sandhurst.

Entered the Royal Engineers.

Served in Palestine, Cyprus and Sudan.

Became a national hero when he successfully led the British army in Sudan and won the victory at Ondurman (1898).

In the Boer war (1899-1902), was appointed chief-of-staff to Lord F. Roberts.

Became Commander-in-Chief in India in 1902 and implemented the reforms to the army.

Military Governor of Egypt (1911-1914) and appointed as secretary of war in 1914.

Recruited three million volunteers to fight Germany.

Drowned when travelling to Russia in 1916.

Gérard LAKE (1744-1808)

Entered the Foot Guards in 1758, gained fast promotions.

Served with his regiment in Germany (1760-1762) and in the Yorktown campaign.

Equerry to the Prince of Wales.

Was appointed to command the Guards Brigade in Flanders in 1793.

Routed the Irish rebels in 1798.

Obtained the command-in-chief in India in 1801.

Defeated the Mahratta Federation led by Scindia and won the great victory of Laswaree, followed by Wellesley's victory at Argaum.

Pursued Holkar and compelled him to surrender at Amritsar.

Returned to England in 1807 where he was made a viscount.

Went to politics and died one year after.

Thomas de LALLY-TOLLENDAL (1702-1766)

Son of an Irish Jacobite emigrated to France.

At the outbreak of the Seven Years War, led a French expedition to India.

Failed in his attempt to capture Madras.

Surrendered to the British in Pondicherry. This defeat put an end to the French ambitions in India.

Returned to France where he was sentenced to death after an unfair trial.

NANA SAHIB (1821-?)

His real name was Dhundu Pant.

The adopted son of the last Peshwa of the Mahratta, his request to the British to grant him the Peshwa's title and pension was refused.

At the outbreak of the Mutiny at Cawnpore (1857), his men massacred the British garrison and colony.

Became a leader of the Mutiny.

After suppression of the rebellion, he escaped to Nepal where he probably died.

In the British popular imagery, he was the archetype of the traitor, killer of women and children, reneged on his own words.

Dighton PROBYN (1833-1924)

Born in London. One of six sons of a naval captain.

In 1849, was gazetted to the 6th Bengal Cavalry.

In 1852, transferred to the 2nd Punjab Cavalry commanded by Sam Browne.

During the Mutiny, won a Victoria Cross in Agra.

Appointed to command 1st Sikh Irregular Cavalry and lead them to China.

In 1866, went to command the Central India Horse.

Was chosen to accompany Queen Victoria's son, as equerry, on his tour to India.

In 1872, he became equerry to the Prince of Wales and his service with the royal family lasted until his death.

RANJIT SINGH (c.1780-1839)

Indian maharajah and warrior. Ruler of the Sikhs.

Seized Lahore (1799) and Amritsar (1809) and expended his territory to the north and west.

Made a treaty with the British, agreeing not to expand south of the Sutlej River.

Built up a formidable army with the help of European officers.

By the time of his death, he controlled all of the Punjab north of the Sutlej as well as Kashmir.

His successors lacked his wisdom and his kingdom fell to Great Britain after the Sikh Wars (1849).

Frederick ROBERTS (1832-1914)

Son of an army General.

Educated at Eton and Sandhurst.

Entered the Bengal Artillery in 1851.

First actions during the siege of Delhi and the relief of Lucknow.

Won the Victoria Cross in 1858.

Took part in peace making on the North West Frontier.

Went to the Abyssinia expedition in 1868.

Appointed quartermaster general of the Indian Army in 1875.

During the second Afghan War, was in command of the Kurram Division.

Commander-in-Chief in India (1885-1893).

Took command of the British forces in South Africa and won the war.

Was made Commander-in-Chief of the British Army. He was the last to bear this title.

RANOJI SCINDIA (1726-1745), also Sindia or Scindhia

Ruler of Gwalior when the Mahratta Peshwa engaged him to command his force there.

The family played an important role, allying at various times with the French and the Mughal rulers.

Defeated by the British, the family was left as titular sovereigns of Gwalior until the partition.

James SKINNER (1778-1841)

British military adventurer.

Son of a lieutenant-colonel and a Rajput lady.

At the age of 18, entered the Mahratta army under de Boigne.

Showed soon military talents and remained in the same service until 1803.

Refused to serve against the British during the first Mahratta War.

Joined Lord Lake and raised a regiment of irregular cavalry which became famous.

Was appointed lieutenant-colonel in 1828 and created a Companion of the Order of the Bath.

Had an intimate knowledge of the character of native Indians and his advice was highly valued by the Governor General.

Owner of vast properties, he ended up his life in a wealthy position.

William SLIM (1897-1970)

Joined the British Army in 1914 as a private.

Was quickly commissioned on the field.

Fought in Gallipoli where he was badly wounded.

Was posted to India in 1919.

Joined the 6th Gurkha Rifles in 1920.

Became head of the "Senior Officers' School" of Belgaum.

Was given command of the 10th Indian Brigade in Sudan.

Wounded in 1941, joined the staff of Wavell in the Middle East.

In March 1942, he commanded all allied troops in Burma.

Forced to withdraw to India.

Commander of the 14th Army, successfully defended Assam and recaptured Burma.

Promoted as commander of Allied Ground Forces in South-East Asia.

Succeeded Montgomery as Chief of the Imperial Staff (1948).

Governor General of Australia (1953).

Died in London in 1970.

TIPU SAHIB (1749-1799)

Sultan of Mysore (1782-1799), son of Haidar Ali.

Fought in his father's campaigns against the British but made peace in 1784.

Invaded Travencore in 1789, provoking a new war.

Defeated in 1792, was forced to cede territory.

A vague alliance with the French gave the Governor General a pretext to invade Mysore in 1798.

Killed when defending his capital at Seringapatam. Mysore was then divided among the victors.

Archibald WAVELL (1883-1950)

Son of a general.

Graduated at the top of his class at Sandhurst.

Fought with distinction in the Boer War and on the India's North West Frontier.

Won the Military Cross at Ypres (1914) but lost his left eye.

Transferred to the Allenby's Staff in Palestine.

Was given the task of creating the Middle East Command and protecting the Suez Canal.

Captured Tobruk from the Italians but failed against the Afrika Korps. Replaced by Auchinleck.

Commanded the British troops in India. Did not get the necessary reinforcements and had to retreat out of Burma.

Promoted to field marshal in 1943 and appointed viceroy the same year.

Replaced by Lord Mountbatten in 1947.

Arthur WELLESLEY (1769-1852)

Better known as the "Iron Duke of Wellington" after his victory of Waterloo.

Attended Eton and the French military school of Angers.

Went into the army in 1787.

Was able to quickly rise to the rank of lieutenant-colonel of the 33rd Foot through strategic use of the purchase system (1794).

Fought with his regiment in Flanders.

Sent to India where his older brother was Governor General.

Gained fame by leading the capture of Seringapatam and the victory of Assaye in 1803.

Returned to England and dabbled in politics but back to active service in 1807.

Took command of the British Army in the Iberian Peninsula in 1809 and drove the French out of Spain.

Was lauded as a hero after Waterloo.

Returned to politics and served as Prime Minister from 1828 to 1830. He was a notably unpopular politician.

Orde WINGATE (1903-1944)

Son of an army officer.

Graduated from Woolwich in 1923 and commissioned in the Royal Artillery.

Served five years in the Sudan Defence Force (1928-1933).

In 1936, joined the Intelligence Staff in Palestine, leading raids against Arab terrorist bases.

Wounded in 1938, served under Wavell in the Middle East Command.

Sent to Khartoum where he formed the Gideon Force, raiding against Italian units on the Abyssinian border.

Joined Wavell in India, was allowed to form the "Chindits", soldiers trained in guerrilla tactics.

Entered Burma in 1943 to disrupt Japanese communications.

Promoted to major general and given six brigades (3rd Division).

Launched "Operation Thursday" on 5th March 1944, a jungle clearing 200 miles behind Japanese lines, destroying roads, railways, bridges and convoys.

Killed when his plane crashed on 14 March 1944.

Bahadur SHAH ZAFAR (1775-1862)

The last Mughal Emperor of India.

Reduced by the British East India Company to a state of dependance. Had only a symbolic function.

Was chosen by the Mutineers as their leader. Captured in Delhi by Major Hodson.

His dynasty ended with the execution of his sons and grandson by Hodson.

Exiled in Burma where he died.

Was also one of the greatest Urdu poets of India.

Appendix III

Wars and Campaigns of the Indian Army

Mysore	5 wars	1767 – 1781 – 1783 – 1789 – 1799
Rohillas	2	1774 – 1794
Mahrattas	3	1778 – 1803 – 1817
Burma	4	1824 – 1852 – 1885 – 1930
Jats	1	1825
Afghanistan	3	1839 – 1878 – 1919
Baluchistan	1	1839
China	3	1840 – 1857 – 1900
Scinde	1	1843
Gwalior	1	1843
Sikhs	2	1845 – 1848
Persia	1	1856
Mutiny	1	1857
Abyssinia	1	1867
Egypt	1	1882
Sudan	1	1885
Chitral	1	1895
East Africa	1	1896
Malakand	1	1897
Tirah	1	1897
2nd Boer	1	1899
Somaliland	1	1901
N. W. Frontier	1	1914
1st WW	1	1914/18
Waziristan	1	1919
Mesopotamia	1	1919
Moplahs	1	1921
2nd WW	1	1939/45

Appendix IV

The Victoria Cross

The Victoria Cross is the highest award for gallantry. Until 1912, it could not be awarded to native-born members of the Indian Army.

For Indian soldiers, the "Choice" medal to reward bravery was the "Indian Order of Merit". The medal was divided into three classes, the first one being the equivalent of the Victoria Cross for those who were not allowed to get it.

Victoria Cross Recipients

1. Indian Order of Merit 1st Class (after the Mutiny)

NAME	UNIT	DATE	LOCATION
DEORAM DOOBEE	73rd Native Infantry	1858	Indian Mutiny
BAHADUR HEDAYUT ALI	Bengal Police Battalion	1858	Indian Mutiny
SHADIL KHAN	3rd Sikh Cavalry	1858	Indian Mutiny
BURMA DEEN	2nd Central India Horse	1868	Capture of an outlaw
MOWLADAD KHAN	20th Punjab Infantry	1877	Jowaki
FYZTULUB	1st Punjab Infantry	1879	Afghan War
Major PYABB	1st Punjab Infantry	1879	Afghan War
KISHANBIR NAGARKOTI	1/5th Gurkha Rifles	1879 1888	Afghan War (1st award) North West Frontier (2nd award)
DHOWKUL SINGH	3rd Bombay Light Cavalry	1880	Afghan War

2. Victoria Cross

NAME	UNIT	DATE	LOCATION
ABDUL HAFIZ	9th Jat Infantry	1944	Imphal, Assam
ADAMS, James William	Bengal Ecclesiastical Department	1879	Killa Kazi, Afghanistan
ADAMS, Robert	Staff Corps and Corps of Guides	1897	Nawa Kili, India
AGANSING RAI	5th Royal Gurkha Rifles	1944	Bishenpur, Burma (now Myanmar)
AIKMAN, Frederick Robertson	Bengal Native Infantry	1858	Amethi, India
AITKEN, Robert Hope Moncrieff	Bengal Native Infantry	1857	Lucknow, India
ALI HAIDAR	13th Frontier Force Rifles	1945	Fusignano, Italy
ALLMAND, Michael	Indian Armoured Corps	1944	Pin Hmi Road Bridge, Burma (now Myanmar)
ANDREWS, Henry John	Indian Medical Service	1919	Waziristan, India
BADLU SINGH	14th Lancers	1918	River Jordan, Palestine
BAKER, Charles George	Bengal Police Battalion	1858	Suhejnee, Bengal
BHANBHAGTA GURUNG	2nd Gurkha Rifles	1945	Tamandu, Burma (now Myanmar)

NAME	UNIT	DATE	LOCATION
BHANDARI RAM	10th Baluch Regiment	1944	Arakan, Burma (now Myanmar)
BLAIR, James	2nd Bombay Light Cavalry	1857	Neemuch, India
BOISRAGON, Guy Hudleston	Indian Staff Corps	1891	Nilt Fort, India
BROWNE, Samuel James	46th Bengal Native Infantry	1858	Seerporah, India
BRUCE, William Arthur McCrae	59th Scinde Rifles	1914	Givenchy, France
BUCKLEY, John	Commissariat Department (Bengal Est.)	1857	Delhi, India
CAFE, William Martin	56th Bengal Native Infantry	1858	Fort Ruhya, India
CARTER, Herbert Augustine	Mounted Infantry	1903	Jidballi, Somaliland (now Somalia)
CHANNER, George Nicolas	Bengal Staff Corps	1875	Perak, Malaya
CHASE, William St. Lucien	28th Native Infantry	1880	Deh Khoja, Afghanistan
CHATTA SINGH	9th Bhopal Infantry	1916	Battle of the Wadi, Mesopotamia
CHHELU RAM	6th Rajputana Rifles	1943	Djebel Garci, Tunisia
CLOGSTOUN, Herbert Mackworth	19th Madras Native Infantry	1859	Chichumbah, India
COBBE, Alexander Stanhope	Other	1902	Erego, Somaliland (now Somalia)
CONNOLLY, William	Bengal Horse Artillery	1857	Jhelum, India
COOK, John	Bengal Staff Corps	1878	Peiwar Kotal, Afghanistan
COSTELLO, Edmond William	22nd Punjab Infantry	1897	Malakand, India
CREAGH, O'Moore	Bombay Staff Corps	1879	Kam Dakka, Afghanistan
CRIMMIN, John	Bombay Medical Service	1889	Lwekaw, Burma (now Myanmar)
CUBITT, William George	13th Bengal Native Infantry	1857	Chinhut, India
CUMMING, Arthur Edward	12th Frontier Force Regiment	1942	Kuantan, Malaya
DARWAN SING NEGI	39th Garhwal Rifles	1914	Festubert, France
DAUNT, John Charles Campbell	11th Bengal Native Infantry	1857	Chota Behar, India
DE PASS, Frank Alexander	34th Prince Albert Victor's Own Poona Horse	1914	Festubert, France
DIAMOND, Bernard	Bengal Horse Artillery	1857	Bolandshahr, India
DUFFY, Thomas	1st Madras Fusiliers (later The Royal Dublin Fusiliers)	1857	Lucknow, India
DUNDAS, James	Bengal Engineers	1865	Dewan-Giri, India
FAZAL DIN	10th Baluch Regiment	1945	Meiktila, Burma (now Myanmar)
FITZGERALD, Richard	Bengal Horse Artillery	1857	Bolandshahr, India
FITZGIBBON, Andrew	Indian Medical Establishment	1860	Taku Forts, China
FORREST, George	Bengal Veteran Establishment	1857	Delhi, India
FOSBERY, George Vincent	4th Bengal European Regiment	1863	Crag Picquet, India
GAJE GHALE	5th Royal Gurkha Rifles	1943	Chin Hills, Burma (now Myanmar)
GANJU LAMA	7th Gurkha Rifles	1944	Ningthoukhong, Burma (now Myanmar)
GIAN SINGH	15th Punjab Regiment	1945	Kamye, Burma (now Myanmar)
GOBAR SING NEGI	39th Garhwal Rifles	1915	Neuve Chapelle, France
GOBIND SINGH	28th Light Cavalry	1917	Peizieres, France
GOODFELLOW, Charles Augustus	Bombay Engineers	1859	Fort of Beyt, India
GRANT, Charles James William	Indian Staff Corps	1891	Thobal, Burma (now Myanmar)

NAME	UNIT	DATE	LOCATION
GRANT, John Duncan	8th Gurkha Rifles	1904	Gyantse Jong, Tibet
HAMILTON, Walter Richard Pollock	Staff Corps and Corps of Guides	1879	Futtehabad, Afghanistan
HAMMOND, Arthur George	Bengal Staff Corps	1879	Asmai Heights, Afghanistan
HARINGTON, Hastings Edward	Bengal Artillery	1857	Lucknow, India
HILLS, James	Bengal Horse Artillery	1857	Delhi, India
HOME, Duncan Charles	Bengal Engineers	1857	Delhi, India
INNES, James John McLeod	Bengal Engineers	1858	Sultanpore, India
ISHAR SINGH	28th Punjab Regiment	1921	Haidari Kach, India
JARRETT, Hanson Chambers Taylor	26th Bengal Native Infantry	1858	Baroun, India
JENNINGS, Edward	Bengal Artillery	1857	Lucknow, India
JOTHAM, Eustace	Other	1915	Spina Khaisora, India
KAMAL RAM	8th Punjab Regiment	1944	River Gari, Italy
KARAMJEET SINGH JUDGE	15th Punjab Regiment	1945	Meiktila, Burma (now Myanmar)
KARANBAHADUR RANA	3rd Queen Alexandra's Own Gurkha Rifles	1918	El Kefr, Egypt
KAVANAGH, Thomas Henry	Bengal Civil Service	1957	Lucknow, India
KEATINGE, Richard Harte	Bombay Artillery	1858	Chundairee, India
KENNY, William David	39th Garhwal Rifles	1920	Kot Kai, India
KERR, William Alexander	24th Bombay Native Infantry	1857	Kolapore, India
KHUDADAD KHAN	129th Duke of Connaught's Own Baluchis	1914	Hollebeke, Belgium
KULBIR THAPA	3rd Gurkha Rifles	1915	Fauquissart, France
LACHHIMAN GURUNG	8th Gurkha Rifles	1945	Taungdaw, Burma (now Myanmar)
LALA	41st Dogras	1916	El Orah, Mesopotamia
LALBAHADUR THAPA	2nd Gurkha Rifles	1943	Rass-es-Zouai, Tunisia
LAUGHNAN, Thomas	Bengal Artillery	1857	Lucknow, India
LYSTER, Harry Hammon	72nd Bengal Native Infantry	1858	Calpee, India
MACINTYRE, Donald	Bengal Staff Corps	1872	Lalgnoora, India
MACLEAN, Hector Lachlan Stewart	Staff Corps and Corps of Guides	1897	Nawa Kili, India
MAHONEY, Patrick	1st Madras Fusiliers (later The Royal Dublin Fusiliers)	1857	Mungulwar, India
MALCOLMSON, John Grant	3rd Bombay Light Cavalry	1857	Battle of Khoosh-ab, Persia
MANGLES, Ross Lowis	Bengal Civil Service	1857	Arrah, India
MAXWELL, Francis Aylmer	Indian Staff Corps	1900	Korn Spruit, South Africa
McDONELL, William Fraser	Bengal Civil Service	1857	Arrah, India
McGOVERN, John	1st Bengal Fusiliers (later The Royal Munster Fusiliers)	1857	Delhi, India
McGUIRE, James	1st Bengal Fusiliers (later The Royal Munster Fusiliers	1857	Delhi, India
McINNES, Hugh	Bengal Artillery	1857	Lucknow, India
MELLISS, Charles John	Indian Staff Corps	1900	Obassa, Ashanti (now Ghana)
MEYNELL, Godfrey	12th Frontier Force Regiment	1935	Mohmand, India
MILLER, James	Bengal Ordnance Depot	1857	Futtehpore, India

NAME	UNIT	DATE	LOCATION
MIR DOST	55 Coke's Rifles (Frontier Force)	1915	Wieltje, Belgium
MOORE, Arthur Thomas	3rd Bombay Light Cavalry	1857	Battle of Khoosh-ab, Persia
NAMDEO JADAV	5th Mahratta Light Infantry	1945	Senio River, Italy
NAND SINGH	Sikh Regiment	1944	Maungdaw-Buthidaung Road, Burma (now Myanmar)
NETRABAHADUR THAPA	5th Royal Gurkha Rifles	1944	Bishenpur, Burma (now Myanmar)
OLPHERTS, William	Bengal Artillery	1857	Lucknow, India
PARK, James	Bengal Artillery	1857	Lucknow, India
PARKASH SINGH	8th Punjab Regiment	1943	Donbaik, Burma (now Myanmar)
PHILLIPPS, Everard Aloysius Lisle	Bengal Native Infantry	1857	Delhi, India
PITCHER, Henry William	4th Punjab Infantry	1863	Crag Picquet, India
PRAKASH SINGH	13th Frontier Force Rifles	1945	Kanlan Ywathit, Burma (now Myanmar)
PREMINDRA SINGH BHAGAT	Corps of Indian Engineers	1941	Gallabat, Abyssinia (now Ethiopia)
PRENDERGAST, Harry North Dalrymple	Madras Engineers	1857	Mundisore, India
PROBYN, Dighton MacNaghton	2nd Punjab Cavalry	1857	Battle of Agra, India
RAM SARUP SINGH	1st Punjab Regiment	1944	Kennedy Peak, Burma (now Myanmar)
RAYNOR, William	Bengal Veteran Establishment	1857	Delhi, India
RENNY, George Alexander	Bengal Horse Artillery	1857	Delhi, India
RICHHPAL RAM	6th Rajputana Rifles	1941	Keren, Eritrea
RIDGEWAY, Richard Kirby	Bengal Staff Corps	1879	Konoma, India
ROBERTS, Frederick Sleigh	Bengal Artillery	1858	Khodagunge, India
RODDY, Patrick	Bengal Army	1958	Kuthirga, India
ROLLAND, George Murray	1st Bombay Grenadiers	1903	Daratoleh, Somaliland (now Somalia)
ROSAMUND, Matthew	Bengal Native Infantry	1857	Benares, India
RYAN, John	1st Madras Fusiliers (later The Royal Dublin Fusiliers)	1857	Lucknow, India
SALKELD, Philip	Bengal Engineers	1857	Delhi, India
SARTORIUS, Reginald William	6th Bengal Cavalry	1874	Abogu, Ashanti (now Ghana)
SCOTT, Andrew	Bengal Staff Corps	1877	Quetta, India
SHAHAMAD KHAN	89th Punjab Regiment	1916	Beit Ayeesa, Mesopotamia
SHEBBEARE, Robert Haydon	60th Bengal Native Infantry	1857	Delhi, India
SHER BAHADUR THAPA	9th Gurkha Rifles	1944	San Marino, Italy
SHER SHAH	16th Punjab Regiment	1945	Kyeyebyin, Burma (now Myanmar)
SINTON, John Alexander	Indian Medical Service	1916	Orah Ruins, Mesopotamia
SMITH, J.	1st Madras Fusiliers (later The Royal Dublin Fusiliers)	1857	Lucknow, India
SMITH, John	Bengal Sappers and Miners	1857	Delhi, India
SMITH, John Manners	Indian Staff Corps	1891	Nilt Fort, India
SMYTH, John George	15th Ludhiana Sikhs	1915	Richebourg L'Aouve, France
THACKERAY, Edward Talbot	Bengal Engineers	1857	Delhi, India
THAMAN GURUNG	5th Royal Gurkha Rifles	1944	Monte San Bartolo, Italy
THOMAS, Jacob	Bengal Artillery	1857	Lucknow, India
TOMBS, Henry	Bengal Horse Artillery	1857	Delhi, India

NAME	UNIT	DATE	LOCATION
TRAVERS, James	2nd Bengal Native Infantry	1857	Indore, India
TREVOR, William Spottiswoode	Bengal Engineers	1865	Dewan-Giri, India
TULBAHADUR PUN	6th Gurkha Rifles	1944	Mogaung, Burma (now Myanmar)
TYTLER, John Adam	66th Bengal Native Infantry	1858	Choorpoorah, India
UMRAO SINGH	Royal Indian Artillery	1944	Kaladan Valley, Burma (now Myanmar)
VOUSDEN, William John	5th Punjab Cavalry	1879	Asmai Heights, Afghanistan
WALKER, William George	4th Gurkha Rifles	1903	Daratoleh, Somaliland (now Somalia)
WALLER, William Francis Frederick	25th Bombay Light Infantry	1858	Gwalior, India
WATSON, John	1st Punjab Cavalry	1857	Lucknow, India
WHEELER, George Campbell	9th Gurkha Rifles	1917	Shumran, Mesopotamia
WHEELER, George Godfrey Massy	7th Hariana Lancers	1915	Shaiba, Mesopotamia
WHITCHURCH, Harry Frederick	Indian Medical Service	1895	Chitral Fort, India
WOOD, John Augustus	20th Bombay Native Infantry	1856	Bushire, Persia
YESHWANT GHADGE	5th Mahratta Light Infantry	1944	Upper Tiber Valley, Italy

Native Sovereigns and Geographical Sites

Khan	mainly Afghanistan
Maharajah	mainly Rajasthan
Nawab	mainly Mysore
Nizam	mainly Hyderabad
Peshwa	mainly Mahratta
Rajah	mainly Rajasthan
Rao	mainly Bengal

	Main cities
Bengal	Calcutta – Benares
Carnatic	Madras
Mahratta	Indore – Gwalior
Mysore	Bengalore
Orissa	Cuttack
Oudh	Lucknow
Punjab	Lahore
Sindh	Karachi
Sutlej	Tributary of the Indus River, Punjab border
United Provinces	United provinces of Agra and Oudh, corresponded approximately to the present-day Indian states of Uttar Pradesh

Bibliography

General Military History

Farwell B., *Armies of the Raj*, Viking 1990.

Longer V., *Red coat to olive green 1600-1974*, Allied publishers, Bombay, 1974.

Mason P., *A matter of Honour*, Jonathan Cape, 1975.

Menzies S. L., *Fidelity and Honour – The Indian Army*, Viking (Penguin India), 1993.

Mollo B., *The Indian Army*, Poole, Blandford, 1981.

Mollo B., *Soldiers of the Raj*, National Army Museum, 1997.

Richards W., *Her Majesty 's army*, vol.3, Virtue and Co, 1890.

Early units

Williams J., *The Bengal native infantry (1810)*, Facsmile, Frederic Muller, 1970.

Harfiel A., *The Indian Army of the Empress* (1861-1903), Spellmount, 1990.

In depth regimental histories

Gaylor J., *Sons of John company*, Spellmount, 1992.

Jackson D., *India's army*, Sampson Low, Marston & Co, 1940.

Uniforms

Carman W. Y., *Indian Army uniforms – Cavalry*, Leonard Hill, 1961.

Carman W. Y., *Indian Army uniforms – Infantry*, Morgan Grampians, 1969.

India Office and Lucker W. Jr., *Our Indian Army*, Adam bros & Shard low, 1919.

Mᶜ Munn G. & Lovett A. C., *The armies of India*, Adams & Charles Black, 1911.

Poulsom L. W., *Buttons of the Indian Army (cavalry)*, Military Press International, 1998.

Osprey Men at Arms:

n° 31, 30th Punjabis;

n° 41, Gurkhas;

n° 67, Indian Mutiny;

n° 72, North West Frontier;

n° 91, Bengal Cavalry Rgts, 1857-1914;

n° 92, Indian infantry Rgts, 1860-1914.

Osprey Elite:

n° 49, The Gurkhas;

n° 75, The Indian Army.

Second World War

Yeats Brown R., *Martial India*, Eyre and Spotiswoode, 1945.

Elliot J. G., *A Roll of Honour*, Cassell, 1965.

indian races and classes

Mᶜ Munn G., *The martial races of India*, Sampson Low, Marston & Co, 1934.

Mᶜ Munn G., *Indian States and Princes*, Jarrolds, 1936.

His Majesty's Stationery Office, *Our Indian Empire*, Harrison & Sons, 1913.

Elite troops

Praval K. C., *India's paratroopers*, Leo Cooper, 1975.

Magazines

Durbar, journal of the Indian military historical society.
Militaria magazine, n°s 196, 198, 202, 204, 207, 209 and 211.
Tradition: Belmont Maitland, special issues, Indian Cavalry.